# STANMORE PAST

First published 1998
by Historical Publications Ltd
32 Ellington Street, London N7 8PL

**ISBN 0948667 49 4**
British Library Cataloguing-in-Publication Data
A catalogue record for this book is available from the British Library


Typeset in Palatino by Historical Publications
Reproduction by G & J Graphics, London EC2
Printed in Zaragoza by Edelvives

# Acknowledgements

No local historian can uncover the history of a specific place without the help of librarians and archivists and older residents. I should like to acknowledge help received from Bob Thompson of Harrow Civic Centre Library for general assistance in finding information and for making photographs available for reproduction from the archives; and the staff of London Metropolitan Archives. Humphrey Ward has always been happy to discuss ideas and has been generous in supplying photocopies of materials. Alf Porter of the Stanmore & Harrow Local History Society has kindly lent several photographs from his personal collection. Other members of the Society have published useful articles over the years in the Society's newsletter. The late Percy Davenport copied the manor court rolls, which have since been lost, and other documents relating to the Stanmores, with scrupulous care, about 70 years ago. To all these people I should like to express my gratitude. Finally I should like to thank my husband, Colin, who has always supported my researches and helped with suggestions and proof-reading.

# The Illustrations

Most of the illustrations are reproduced by kind permission of the London Borough of Harrow and others were supplied by the author. We would also like to thank the following:

Aerofilms: *66, 89, 195*

Cadland Settled Estates: *132*

Stephen A. Castle and the *London Archaeologist: 9*

Country Life: *21, 22*

Guildhall Library, Lysons extra-illustrated edition: *131*

Harrow Observer: *45, 143*

London Metropolitan Archives: *99*

Alf Porter: *14, 15, 61, 142, 146, 147*

Yale Centre for British Art, Paul Mellon Collection: *130*

# STANMORE PAST

by Eileen M. Bowlt

HISTORICAL PUBLICATIONS

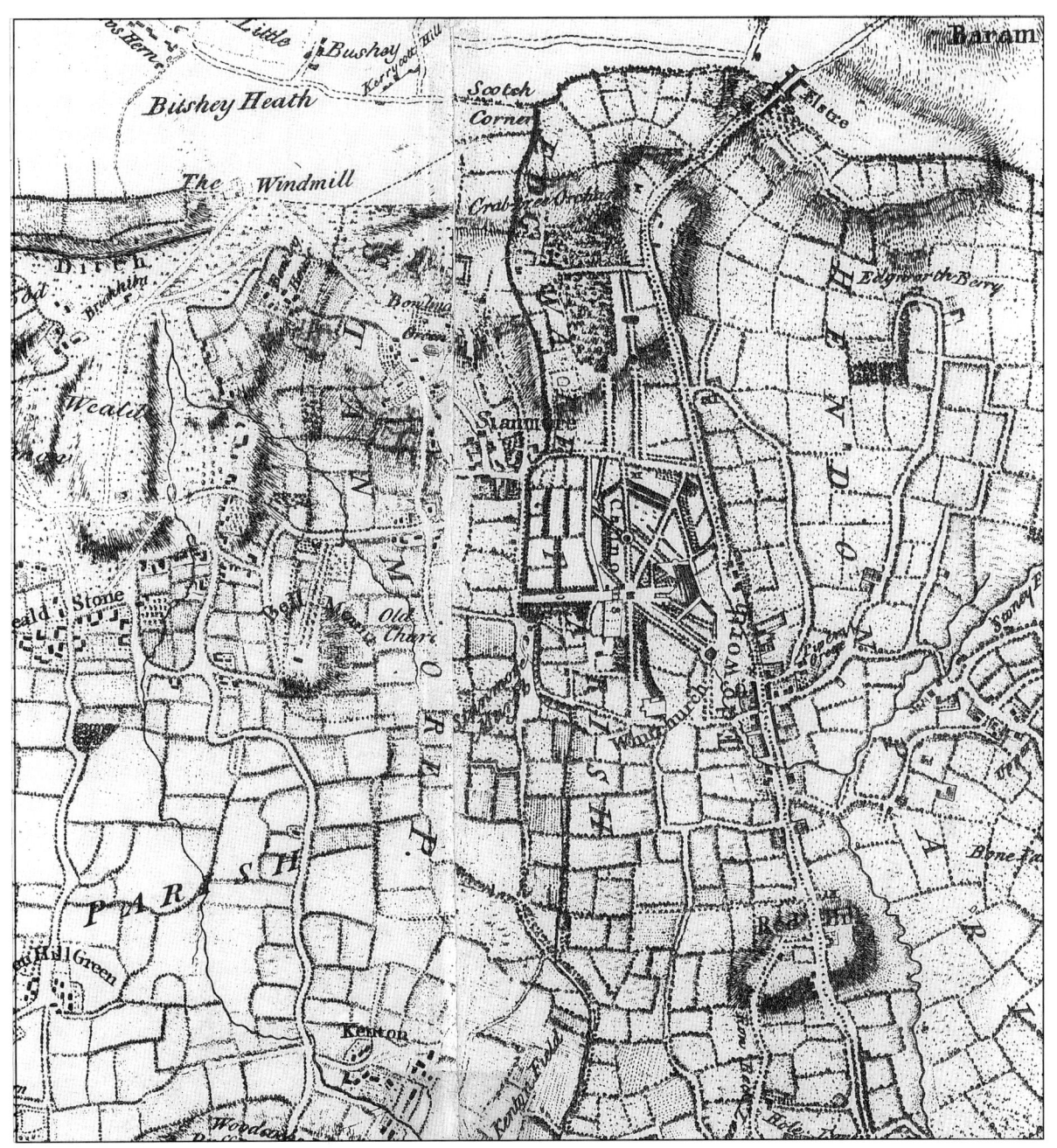

*1. Great and Little Stanmore as depicted on John Rocque's map of Middlesex, 1754.*

2.  *High Street, Edgware c.1890, looking south towards London.  The right hand side of the street is Little Stanmore, the left hand is Edgware.  The Masons' Arms on the extreme right is on the corner of Whitchurch Lane.  The inn sign in the centre of the picture hangs from the Chandos Arms.*

# Early Times

Stanmore, lying between the Edgware Road on the east and Harrow on the west, and stretching northwards from Kingsbury to the Middlesex/Hertfordshire county boundary, is now regarded as one of London's leafier and more desirable suburbs. The proximity of London and easy access to it via the major route on the east, (originally laid out by the Romans as Watling Street), accounts for Stanmore's attractiveness as a rural retreat for London citizens and men of affairs from medieval times onwards, but it was essentially an agricultural area.

In the eighteenth and nineteenth centuries elaborate houses like Canons, Stanmore Park and Bentley Priory, were built or rebuilt and developed and surrounded by extensive parkland, casting an air of tranquillity and opulence around the village and unintentionally providing a suitable setting for twentieth-century suburban inhabitants who want to feel that they are living in the country. What can better give an illusion of pastoral life in the late 1990s than to stroll among the long-horned cattle grazing in the grounds of Bentley Priory before jumping on a train or creeping down a motorway to go to work?

Stanmore is situated on the hilly northern slopes of Middlesex which rise to more than 400ft above sea-level at the common and Brockley Hill, but roll away to become flat, and in some places marshy land, south of the Uxbridge Road, except for Belmont at the southern end of Stanmore golf course. Most of the topsoil is London clay with small areas of Claygate sand and pebble gravel on the hilltop ridge. The relief of the area and the soil have in some measure dictated the way the land has been utilised over the centuries. Woodland that once covered most of north-west Middlesex remains on the steeper slopes, while the level ground, where ploughs could work more easily, had become arable fields during the Middle Ages.

## MANORS AND PARISHES

The rectangle of land that is Stanmore was divided longitudinally into two manors before the Norman Conquest and ecclesiastically into two parishes soon after 1130. Great Stanmore is on the west and Little Stanmore on the east. The division between the two ran north to south from the county boundary, east of Dennis Lane and west of Cloisters Wood, then down Marsh Lane, and parallel to, but some way east of Honeypot Lane. The marsh straddled the boundary, but was finally agreed to be in Great Stanmore in the nineteenth

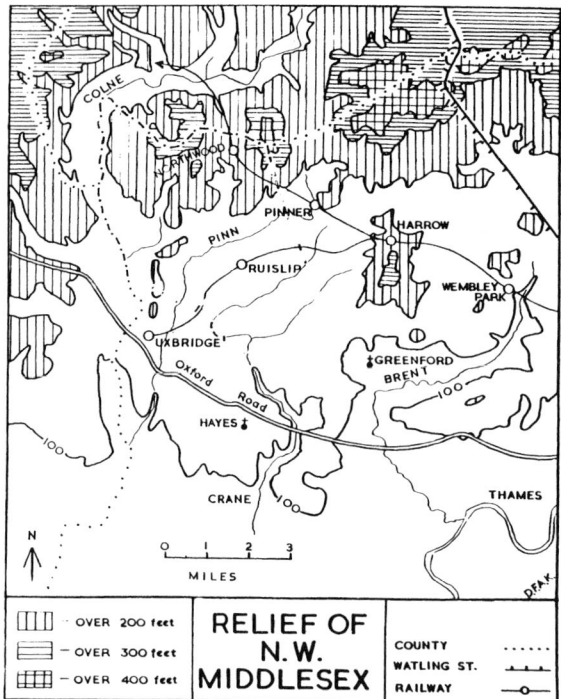

*3. Relief map of north-west Middlesex showing the high ground on Stanmore Common (after D.F.A. Kiddle).*

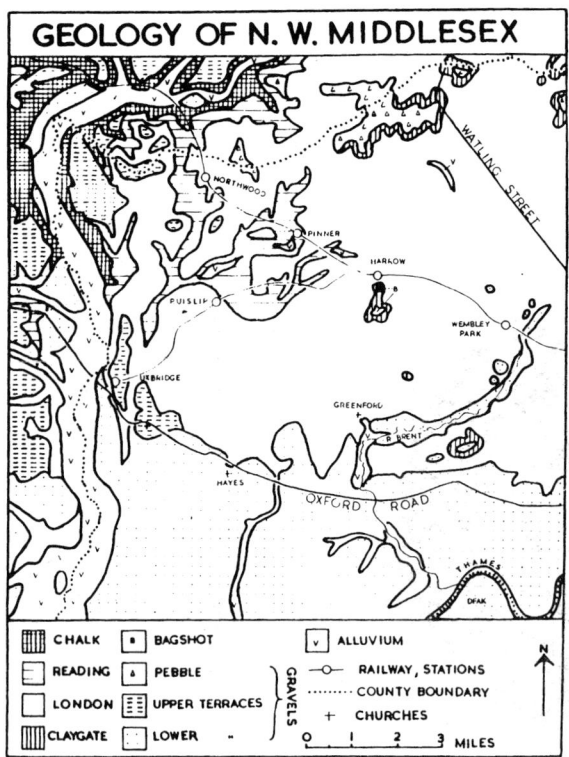

*4. The geology of north-west Middlesex showing Claygate sand and pebble on Stanmore Common (after D.F.A. Kiddle).*

century. Both parishes were crossed by roads from Watling Street: to Watford and to Uxbridge. The Watford road left Watling Street at Stone Grove in medieval times and traversed Little Stanmore diagonally to join the top of Stanmore Hill and continue across Stanmore Common. James Brydges, later 1st Duke of Chandos, diverted it to go around the park of his new mansion, Canons, in 1718, improving the old track that led from Watling Street to Uxbridge at the same time in compensation. The old track became the new London Road and joined the way to Uxbridge at the bottom of Dennis Lane. Wood Lane joined the road across the common that eventually went to Watford. South-west of Green Lane the road to Uxbridge was called Colliers Lane, suggestive of charcoal burning in the area.

Both Great and Little Stanmore, along with Harrow, Kingsbury and Hendon, were in the Hundred of Gore, an administrative division of Middlesex that had been established in late Saxon times. During the medieval period representatives of each vill would have had to attend the Hundred court regularly, whose open-air meeting place was in Kingsbury, where the Police Cadet Training College now stands. Both Stanmores became part of Hendon Rural District in 1895, the

Harrow Urban District in 1934 and subsequently part of the London Borough of Harrow.

## LITTLE STANMORE

Little Stanmore had a manor house, where Canons was later built, and a medieval church close by, detached from the main settlement that was on Watling Street. The lane now called Whitchurch Lane ran to the church and the marsh. The major road from London was an obvious place for a hamlet to develop, but the fact that Watling Street was also the boundary between Little Stanmore and Edgware, gave rise to the anomaly of the road at that point being called Edgware High Street and the houses and inns on the Little Stanmore side being considered to be in Edgware. Rocque's 1754 map of Middlesex (*ill. 1*) compounds the error by showing it as Edg*worth* and labelling Little Stanmore parish as Edg*ware* Parish. At the northern end of the parish the village of Elstree also straddles Watling Street, a small portion actually being in Little Stanmore. The heathland up there was called Bushey Heath. Apart from these settlements there were scarcely any other houses in Little Stanmore before the twentieth century.

5. *These cottages in Elstree High Street (now demolished) were actually in Little Stanmore parish. The facades were modern additions.*

Rocque's map shows an unnamed lane running south from the church towards Roe Green in Kingsbury. This was actually Bacon Lane, with a branch off to Watling Street on the line of the modern Bacon Lane. There is no evidence of common fields in Little Stanmore after the medieval period. (*See p43*).

## GREAT STANMORE
The church and manor house of Great Stanmore in medieval times were down Old Church Lane, near the common fields, but a new church (now the ruined old church) was built in 1632 just north of Colliers Lane, probably because most of the houses were by then congregated near the bottom of Green Lane, Stanmore Hill and Dennis Lane, with more on the higher ground near the common, in fact practically all north of the cross route. Colliers Lane was diverted to the present line of the Uxbridge Road about 1800 by the Drummonds of Stanmore Park. Green Lane and its southern continuation, Old Church Lane, had originally led directly to the medieval village. Stanmore Hill forked off Green Lane, perhaps a short cut from Watford to London, after the new London Road was improved by James Brydges.

## BRITISH TRIBES AND GRIM'S DITCH
An obelisk stands in the grounds of the Royal National Orthopaedic Hospital on Brockley Hill with Latin inscriptions, which were translated by Walter Druett.[1] The information is largely fanciful, saying that a fortress of the Suellani tribe who, under the leadership of Cassivellaunus, put the Romans to flight at the time of Caesar's invasion in 54 BC, stood close by. William Sharpe, who lived at Brockley Hill House and was Secretary to the Duke of Chandos, erected it in the mid-eighteenth century. In fact, Caesar described defeating Cassivellaunus at a stronghold defended by a rampart and ditch in a densely wooded area, which is conjectured to have been Wheat-hampstead. Sharpe also seems to have thought that the ridge above Stanmore marked the bound-

6. *William Sharpe's obelisk in the grounds of the Royal National Orthopaedic Hospital.*

*7. Grim's Dyke at Grim's Dyke Golf Club, Harrow Weald.*

*8. Pottery found at Brockley Hill in the 1930s.*

ary between the lands of the British tribes, the Catuvellauni and the Trinobantes.

Nearby in Pear Wood there are a bank and ditch, thought to be a continuation of Grim's Ditch, the massive earthwork running through neighbouring Harrow Weald. Some antiquarians have suggested that Grim's Ditch marked an Iron Age tribal boundary, while others have suggested that it is Saxon and indicates the southernmost territory of Offa of Mercia, to whom is attributed Offa's Dyke on the Welsh border. A boundary seems the most likely explanation of such an earthwork as it is not very well placed for defensive purposes, but efforts to date it have so far proved inconclusive. Excavations near the Grims Dyke Hotel at Harrow Weald in 1979 found little dating evidence, except for a hearth within the bank, which had been used for only a short period (a radio-carbon date of AD 50, plus or minus 80) presumably at the time of construction. The date fits in with Belgic and Iron Age pottery found in the same earthwork at Pinner Green in 1957.[2] This evidence supports the tribal boundary hypothesis. The name Grim, meaning devil, is Saxon and could well have been given by the Saxons who came upon the ditch, believing it to be the work of the devil. The Pear Wood bank and ditch seem to have been constructed separately and later than Grim's Ditch as digs there between 1948 and 1973 discovered 4th century AD material at the bottom of the north bank.[3] It was probably connected with the early Saxon invasions. There was also early Roman material on the site.

## THE ROMANS IN STANMORE

The Antonine Itinerary refers to a town called *Sulloniacae* lying twelve miles from *Londinium* and nine from *Verulamium* (St Albans). William Camden writing in his *Britanniae* (1586), observed that the site of *Sulloniacae* was probably on

Brockley Hill rather than at Chipping Barnet as had previously been thought. Much effort has been expended in trying to find the site during the last ninety years or so, starting in 1909. An exploratory dig by the London & Middlesex Archaeological Society, under the leadership of H.S. Braun, was undertaken in September 1937 on the east side of Watling Street opposite the grounds of the Royal National Orthopaedic Hospital. More excavations took place on both sides of Watling Street in and south of the Hospital grounds between 1947 and 1977, being annual events from 1971, when the Brockley Hill Excavations Field Work Group was directed by Stephen Castle. It was hoped to find the site of *Sulloniacae* and establish the route of the Roman Watling Street. A two-week dig took place in February 1995 at the former Wimpey Sports Ground, immediately south of the earlier excavated areas and subsequently a watching brief was undertaken to determine whether evidence of the Roman road or any wayside settlement remained lower down the hill.

From all these digs it is concluded that Roman Watling Street ran west of the present A5 and varied in width from 13 to 25 ft. It had a metalled surface and a clay bank. The bank was apparently constructed between the 1st and mid-2nd century AD and appears to have been in use until the

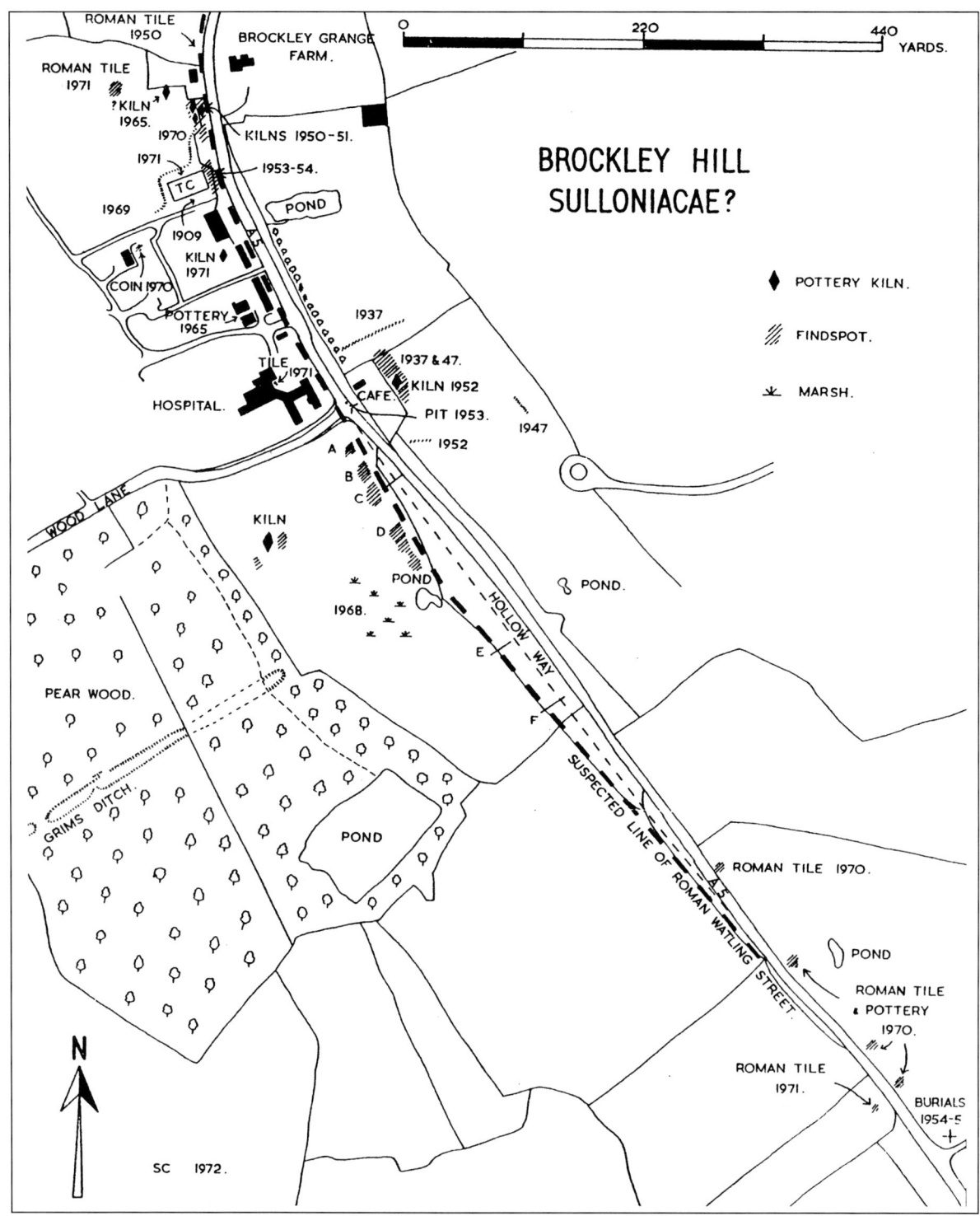

9.  *Map showing archaeological finds on or near Brockley Hill from 1937 to 1971 (reproduced by permission from the London Archaeologist, Spring 1972, vol. 1, no. 14).*

fourth century. The present road was laid out in 1827. South of the Hospital grounds there was evidence of an eighteenth-century hollow way between the Roman road and the A5.[4]

Whether *Sulloniacae* has been found or not is uncertain. A substantial pottery was certainly flourishing here on Watling Street in the 1st and 2nd century AD, producing domestic pots of various kinds – mortaria, flagons, beakers and so on. Fourteen kilns that were working between 50 and 160 AD have been excavated, and the mortaria stamps show the names of thirty potters, some of whose work has also been found at Radlett and elsewhere. The position on a main road would have provided easy access to markets. Ample water and clay were to be found on the hill top where there were several springs and streams. Clay was dug and the pits were then backfilled with debris from the kilns. The finds were of a granular fabric, some with cream slip, and a fine-textured red pottery was produced after 110-20 AD. The kilns must have been situated in or near a village of some sort, but no evidence of a town with planned buildings and streets has come to light. Remains of cobbled floors laid in the late third/early fourth century and such finds as a brooch, a pin, a fastener, black burnished ware and some coins of the fourth century, show that there was some occupation after the pottery production ended in the mid-second century at a time of growing competition from potters in Oxford and Warwickshire.[5] Two second-century cremation burials found at the corner of Brockley Hill and Pipers Green Lane also indicate a domestic site. The Antonine Itinerary gives no indication of the size of *Sulloniacae*. It is possible that the pottery village also had an inn, not yet discovered, that served as a posting station. In any event the settlement did not survive beyond the fourth century and there is no evidence of continuity of habitation on the site.

## SAXON STANMORE

Stanmore, meaning 'stony mere' (or pool), is first mentioned in a document of 793, when Offa, King of Mercia, granted a number of lands, including ten holdings in Stanmore, to the Abbey of St Albans that he refounded in that year.[6] This suggests that there were ten farms in the area by the late eighth century, if nothing else. At some time between 957 and 1066 Stanmore had been divided into two parts and seems to have been taken into the king's hands. A charter dated 957, giving the boundaries of Lotheresleaghe in Hendon and Tunworth in Kingsbury, implies that St Alban's lands then extended as far south as the Kingsbury boundary and so still included Stanmore.[7]

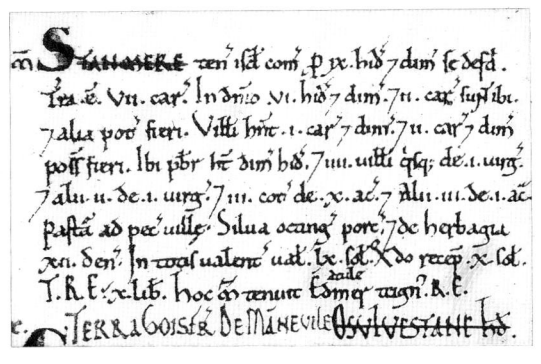

*10. Great Stanmore in the Domesday Book.*

The next definite information comes from two entries in the Domesday Book 1086 where two manors written as *Stanmere* and *Stanmera* are listed as the holdings of Robert Count of Mortain and Roger de Rames respectively. The Count of Mortain's land became Great Stanmore and Roger's manor was later called Little Stanmore. Just why the area was split is unknown, but the division was made before the Conquest, for the Domesday survey gives the names of Edmund Atule, a thegn of Edward the Confessor and Algar, Earl Harold's man, as owners of the separate parts in the time of King Edward. The royal connections suggest that these men received a divided Stanmore as gifts of the king rather than the Abbey. Kingsbury, once a royal estate, was also in the hands of one of Edward's thegns, Wlward Wit. Edmund Atule was a man of substance, having widespread property at Berkhampstead in Hertfordshire and in Devon and Somerset, as well as in Middlesex. His Norman successor, Robert, Count of Mortain, was half brother of William the Conqueror, with many estates in distant counties. His manors in Buckinghamshire, Hertfordshire and Middlesex were joined to form the Honor of Berkhampstead, where there was a castle. Roger de Rames who succeeded to Algar's lands held other property, mainly in Essex and Suffolk.

A comparison of the two parts of Stanmore as they were in 1086 is illuminating and suggests that the original area had been cut almost exactly in half as can be seen from the table on the next page.

In the Domesday Survey of 1086, both Stanmores were said to have enough land for seven ploughs to till. But in both only about half the land was actually being worked, which perhaps suggests under-population. The thirteen people listed at Great Stanmore and the twelve in Little Stanmore were all probably heads of households. If one

| STANMERE (Great Stanmore) | STANMERA (Little Stanmore) |
|---|---|
| 9½ hides, land for 7 ploughs | 9½ hides, land for 7 ploughs |
| 6½ acres in demesne | 4 acres in demense |
| 2 ploughs on demesne could be 1 more | 1 plough on demesne, could be 2 more |
| The villeins have 1½ ploughs | The villeins have 3 ploughs |
| They could have 2½ more | They could have 1 more |
| 6 villeins | 9 villeins |
| 6 cottars | 3 bordars |
| 1 priest | 2 slaves |
| Woodland for 800 pigs | Woodland for 800 pigs |
| Pasture | Pasture |
| Value AD1086  60 shillings | 60 shillings |
| Value AD1066-7 10 shillings | 10 shillings |
| Time of King Edward  £10 | £10 |

suggests that the average household size, including slaves and servants, was 4.5, then Great Stanmore had about 58 people, while Little Stanmore had 54, just over a hundred altogether, giving us a very sparsely populated ground, considering that the actual area was the same as that of Stanmore in the early twentieth century. Perhaps there had been more people living there before the Conquest.

Domesday also showed that the value of the two Stanmores had dropped considerably since the Conquest. In the time of King Edward the manors were valued at £10 each, but had declined to a mere ten shillings apiece (a 95% drop) when the new Norman owners took them over about 1067, suggesting that something catastrophic had happened in 1066, perhaps devastating the farms and inhabitants. The other manors in the Hundred of Gore also went down in value – Harrow by 66.6%, Kingsbury by 50% and Hendon by 33.3% – but nowhere near so drastically as the Stanmores. Possibly the Normans passing down Watling Street from Berkhampstead in the late autumn of 1066 on their way to crown William at Westminster, camped at Stanmore, seized the crops and laid waste the land, or maybe the people of Stanmore rebelled against the invaders and were savagely repressed.

## THE LOCAL COMMUNITY

The hundred or so men, women and children living in the two manors in 1086 must mostly have lived off the land. The villeins were the highest class of dependent peasants in the village community. Five of them in Stanmore had a virgate of land each and another ten held half a virgate each. A virgate, depending on local conditions and custom, amounted to about thirty acres. Below the villeins on the economic scale came the bordars or smallholders. The three in Stanmore had five acres each. The cottars, below them, were indeed cottagers with small pieces of land. Of the six listed, three shared ten acres between them and the other three shared just one acre. They would have been the poorer members of the community, but craftsmen such as blacksmith and carpenter may also have been found among the cottars, needing less land than the villeins because they made a living by their trades.

Higher in the social scale than the villeins ranked the one priest, noted on the Great Stanmore manor. No place in Middlesex is said to have a church in the Domesday Survey, but there are a number of priests mentioned and it is assumed that churches existed to go with them. As Harrow, Hendon and Kingsbury also had priests, it appears likely that the parish of Stanmore embraced both the Stanmore manors. A church was built in Little Stanmore before 1130 by the de Rames family.

Both manors together had enough woodland to support 1600 pigs, which argues a heavily wooded area. The much larger manor of Harrow had woodland for 2,000 pigs, only 20% more. Pasture for the village livestock was available in both manors and payments for grazing brought in two shillings in Little Stanmore and one shilling in Great Stanmore.

# The Manors of Stanmore

## ST ALBAN'S ABBEY AND ST BARTHOLOMEW'S PRIORY

The early Norman holders of the Stanmore lands gave most of them into ecclesiastical ownership. William, the son of Count Robert of Mortain (see p13), restored Great Stanmore to St Albans c1100[1] and the grandsons of Roger de Rames gave portions of Little Stanmore to the Priory of St Bartholomew at West Smithfield soon after 1130.[2] By 1350, after a series of complicated land transactions beyond the scope of this book,[3] the priory had acquired the whole of Little Stanmore and Great Stanmore as well, although it was agreed in 1392 that the Abbot of St Albans should receive five marks (one mark was worth two-thirds of a pound) whenever a new prior was appointed.[4] St Bartholomew's remained in possession of all its Stanmore lands until the priory was dissolved in 1539 during the Reformation. Being absentee landlords, the priors either leased out parcels of the estate, often for periods of thirty years, or put stewards in charge.

## EARLY MANOR HOUSES
### Great Stanmore

The manor house or hall of Great Stanmore stood within a moat near to the medieval parish church. The church was on the north side of Wolverton Road and the hall just to the south. The moat is shown on maps into modern times, squarish in shape, with an oval island. It was fed by a leat from the Stanburn brook and was complete on the map accompanying the Stanmore Tithe Award in 1838, but had only two arms on the 1865 Ordnance Survey map. John, Abbot of St Albans from 1235-60, built a hall in Great Stanmore, but whether or not it was the first on the moated site is unknown.[5] A new manor house was built at the north end of Church Lane towards the end of the sixteenth century.[6] The old manor house probably became a farmhouse, but was replaced by a new

11. *The Manor House at the top of Old Church Lane, which was built there before the end of the sixteenth century. Over the years the house acquired a brick facade which appears to have been covered with stucco and new windows and bays. In 1664 it was taxed for having 16 hearths. It was demolished in 1930 when Samuel Wallrock created an olde worlde New Manor House, further south in Old Church Lane.*

building on the opposite side of Old Church Lane to the moat before 1800. It is shown on Thomas Milne's land use map of that date.

## Little Stanmore and Canons

St Bartholomew's Priory was a house of Augustinian Canons, which gave rise to an alternative name, 'Canons', for the manor of Little Stanmore. Canons originally applied only to the manor house, but later was often, but not invariably, used for the whole estate. A description of Little Stanmore in 1277,[7] before the whole manor was in the hands of St Bartholomew's, divided Little Stanmore into two estates, Stanmore Chenduit and the land of William Parys. The Chenduit portion took its name from the owner, Stephen Chenduit, and is remembered in the modern Chenduit Road. Both estates had courts (manor houses) each with two gardens. As the Chenduit land stretched down into Kingsbury, the court may well have been in the southern part of Little Stanmore, where Canons later stood. A field named Wyneberwe became Wimborough and had become an estate in its own right by the sixteenth century. Occasionally it was called a manor and has also had a modern road named after it (Wemborough Road). When the manor house of Canons was leased to William Daunce of Whitchurch in 1535, it had a dove house attached and was surrounded by a moat, well stocked with fish.[8]

## AFTER THE DISSOLUTION

The last prior of St Bartholomew's, Robert Fuller, was permitted to keep the priory's estates in Little Stanmore, but he died very soon after in 1540, when everything reverted to the Crown. Hugh Losse, tenant of the manor house, Canons, obtained a grant for it in 1543 and had bought up most of the other Little Stanmore leases before 1552. He was a London merchant who made a business of buying up former monastic properties after the Reformation. Little Stanmore stayed with his family until 1604, when his grandson sold the whole estate along with the lordship of the manor to Sir Thomas Lake, Secretary of State to James I.[9] Lake presumably rebuilt Canons, as a plan of 1606 in the Sir John Soane Museum is labelled 'Canons, my Lady Lake's house'.[10]

In Great Stanmore, Jeffery Chamber, chief steward of St Bartholomew's, seems to have been another astute businessman who did well out of the fall of the monasteries. He was appointed Surveyor and Receiver-General to the Court of Augmentations which had been set up in 1535, to deal with the monastic properties being taken over by the Crown. Already the prior's bailiff at Great

Stanmore, he took out a 15-year lease on the manor in 1538 and it was granted to him and his heirs in consideration of £400 in 1542. Once in full possession he sold part of it to a Spanish mercenary in the king's service, Pedro de Gamboa, who was granted the whole estate in 1547, a year or two after Chamber's death. He did not last long. The streets of London were not safe, especially perhaps for Spanish mercenaries, and Pedro was murdered by a Fleming near St Sepulchre's in 1550, apparently leaving no male heirs.[11]

After a subsequent series of leaseholders, Sir Thomas Lake came into possession and thus the two manors of Stanmore were united.[12]

## THE LAKES

The Lakes maintained their interests in Stanmore until 1713, proving a very disputatious family. The first Sir Thomas, James I's Secretary of State, died about 1630 and was succeeded by his son, another Sir Thomas. He conveyed Little Stanmore and the mansion Canons, where presumably his widowed mother had been living, to another lady after his mother's death. When Sir Thomas died in 1653 he left as heir his only son, Thomas, then only twelve years old and two daughters besides, Dorothy and Elizabeth. The boy was taken into the custody of two uncles, Sir Lancelot Lake and Sir William Domvill, but while still a minor, without their knowledge, he entered into a marriage with Mary Wroth. William Bokenham, who had married Mary's sister, somehow got the boy into his custody and persuaded him to convey the manor of Great Stanmore to himself. Soon afterwards Thomas Lake came of age, but fell sick of the smallpox and died, leaving William Bokenham in possession; whereupon the sisters Dorothy and Elizabeth exhibited a Bill of Complaint in the Court of Chancery.[13]

Agreement was reached in 1663, with a great part of the demesne lands of Great Stanmore being sold to Sir Lancelot Lake, their uncle at Canons. Each sister was to have £9000. What was left of the Great Stanmore lands and the lordship of the manor remained in the hands of William Bokenham until 1679 when he sold them all to Matthew Smith a London mercer who was dead within two years. A vintner, John Powell following Smith, remained lord until 1700, when John Rogers who was a London goldsmith and had an estate at Bushey, bought the manor.[14]

Meanwhile Canons and Little Stanmore were passing through the generations of Sir Lancelot's family. His second son, Lancelot succeeded in 1680 and he was followed by his nephew, also called Lancelot, in 1689. When this third Lancelot

*12. The eastern elevation of Canons in 1720, by John Price who took over from James Gibbs as architect for the house in 1719.*

died in 1693 his estates passed back a generation to a younger uncle, Warwick Lake.[15]

Lancelot's younger sister, Mary Lake, born in 1666, subsequently married a distant cousin, the young James Brydges, son of Baron Chandos of Sudeley, in 1696. He was soon to be Earl of Carnarvon and in 1719, (six years after Mary's death), Duke of Chandos. Her uncle Warwick sold the mansion house, Canons, and the manor of Little Stanmore and his portion of Great Stanmore, to him in 1709. The two parts of Stanmore were again united when John Rogers sold Great Stanmore to Humphrey Walcot on behalf of James Brydges in 1714.[16]

## JAMES BRYDGES

Despite his youth James Brydges was an assiduous and successful place-seeker, being appointed to the post of paymaster-general to the Duke of Marlborough's forces abroad when little more than thirty years old. He held the post between 1705-1714 and made a substantial fortune thereby. When a government inquiry was made into the enormous expenditure on the army, he was not expelled from his post, though it was said by Smollett that Brydges could account for all of it 'excepting three millions'!

During the early years of his marriage to Mary Lake, he frequently visited her aunts and other relatives at Stanmore and according to his journal played bowls at the bowling green that had been enclosed from the heath long before in 1637. There was already a club house of some kind there, forerunner of the Banqueting House which he built beside the bowling green while he was living at Canons.

*13. The entrance gates to Canons at Stone Grove. The pillars still stand, but bereft of the small lodges.*

## CANONS

Frequently spoken of as 'princely Chandos', Brydges began to build himself a suitable palace at Canons in 1714. He rebuilt the parish church, St Lawrence, Whitchurch, at the same time. This was ready for use in 1716. The house was complete by 1720, including a private chapel decorated by the same artists who had been working on the church, being the last part to be finished. Canons was set in beautifully landscaped grounds, watered by a canal fed from the Spring Pond on the Little Common.

The house was approached by four magnificent avenues. Halfway down the main avenue from Edgware was a basin full of fish, likened by Defoe to the one on the road from Bushey Park to Hampton Court. The entrance gates at Edgware were flanked by great stone pillars, decorated with the Duke's arms and supporters and just inside

*14. A painting by Kneller of the 1st Duke of Chandos with his second wife, Cassandra, about the time of their marriage in 1713. The sons, John and Henry, were the only surviving children from his first marriage.*

*15. The grand lodge at Stone Grove, known as North Lodge and a gentleman's residence in its own right.*

were lodges which housed former soldiers from the Chelsea Hospital, whom he employed as bodyguards and as an entourage to add pomp to his ceremonious lifestyle. Trumpeters are said to have heralded each course at dinner! A house belonging to the Bates family since 1700 was purchased by Brydges in 1716 and pulled down to make way for the main gate.[17] The basin and gate pillars remain, the latter looking rather forlorn and stripped of their embellishments. There is also a Greek temple summer house, much vandalised, in the part of the grounds that is now a public park. The grounds were scattered with lead statues and urns and alive with exotic birds and imported trees and other plants.

Brydges first thought of refronting the existing Canons in brick, but eventually involved many of the distinguished architects of the day in his plans for a new house. James Gibbs, then in his early thirties and working on St Mary-le-Strand at the same time, probably had the largest hand in the design of the Portland stone facades, with John Price continuing Gibbs's work on the north and south fronts. William Talman had already done some work on outbuildings. The house was set around a courtyard and the sides were built in a fairly plain classical style with rustication and columns of the Ionic order. The great length of the front, almost 50 yards, gave it an unbalanced appearance. Nevertheless Daniel Defoe enthused 'The fronts are all of freestone, the columns and pilasters are lofty and beautiful, the windows very high, with all possible ornaments. In a word, the whole structure is built with such a profusion of expense, and all finished with such a brightness of fancy, goodness of judgment; that I can assure you, we see many palaces of sovereign princes abroad, which do not equal it.'[18]

Inside, the house was a repository of the art and sculpture of leading artists and craftsmen of the time: James Thornhill, William Kent, Bellucci and Laguerre; and of treasures from the past, such as cartoons by Raphael. There was splendid carving by Grinling Gibbons. His *Stoning of St Stephen*, made for the library, is now in the Victoria and Albert Museum. The doors had gold or silver locks and hinges. Not everyone appreciated the ostentatious style and Alexander Pope, although he denied it, almost certainly satirised Canons as Timon's villa in his *Epistle on False Taste*. The private chapel particularly impressed Defoe, who wrote that it 'is a singularity not only in its building and the beauty of its workmanship, but in this also, that the Duke maintains here a full choir and has the worship performed there with the best music'.[19]

## HANDEL AT CANONS

During the years 1718-20, before the chapel was complete, Handel was music master at Canons and while there composed twelve Chandos anthems in honour of the Duke, and other works, in one of which, *Pieces pour le Clavacine*, the air of the Harmonious Blacksmith appears. The story

17. *George Frederick Handel.*

16. *The hut outside no. 101 Edgware High Street used to call itself Handel's Smithy, referring to the apocryphal story that Handel while sheltering in a smithy was inspired by the sounds made by the smith's hammer on the anvil, to compose the 'air of the harmonious blacksmith'. The building shown here was erected about 1930 after the demolition of the former barn that stood on this spot. The hut is now a monumental masons.*

18.  *Willam Hallett's Canons as it appeared in 1782.  Much of the material came from the Duke of Chandos's house.*

*19. The basin in Canons Park Drive that survives from the Duke of Chandos's gardens. The water fowl are still attractive, but less exotic than in the Duke's day.*

*20. A temple in Canons Park.*

that Handel, seeking shelter from the rain in a smithy in Edgware High Street, was inspired by the notes made by the hammer striking the anvil and created the tune around them, is attractive, but untrue. The legend was first floated in an anonymous letter published in the *Times* in 1835. It was centred on William Powell, a blacksmith who was not apprenticed until 1725, five years after Handel had left Canons. A notice was fixed to the old smithy and copies of the music were sold to the curious. As a result of the interest taken in the story a wooden memorial was put up in the graveyard at St Lawrence's where William Powell had been buried in 1780. Such was the appeal of the story or the increased trade engendered by it, that in 1850 the graveboard was replaced by a stone, which has recently been renewed. The legend dies hard! Handel's masque *Haman and Mordecai* was produced in the private theatre at Canons in 1720 and some twelve years later was developed into the oratorio, *Esther*.

*21. Canons in 1920. Sir Arthur Du Cros, founder of the Dunlop Rubber Company, employed Charles E. Mallows to add a storey and extend the east side. A new screen gave privacy to the main entrance on the south front.*

*22. The new hall at Canons furnished for Sir Arthur Du Cros.*

## THE CHANDOS ESTATE

The Duke of Chandos owned some 1492 acres in Little Stanmore by 1730, having purchased the lands piecemeal. He acquired several inns, two along the Stanmore side of Edgware High Street: the Crown (otherwise known as Pages) in 1715 from John Thompson, the Flower de Luce from Brian Pooley in 1717 and the Rose & Crown at Stanmore Marsh from John Friend and his wife in 1716.[20] The Rose & Crown had been erected on common land at Stanmore Marsh by Harry Bunn sometime before 1695. Several other cottages and lands were bought up as well, including one that had been an inn called the Axe & Gate at Smith's Hill, Edgware. The demesne land (that portion of the manor retained by the lord of the manor) of Great Stanmore amounted to 208 acres in 1714[21] and comprised the manor house and lands, the Warren House with the Coney Warren on the common and other lands, the Bowling

Green House, with the bowling green and a number of fields. The manor house at the top of Old Church Lane was assessed as having sixteen hearths in the 1664 Hearth Tax Returns and was always leased out. The Earl of Carnarvon, as Brydges then was, had 778 acres altogether in Great Stanmore.

Many parts of the estate were leased out for 21-year periods. A lease granted to Thomas Wrench, blacksmith, from 12 April 1738, is typical. The property, amounting to just over an acre, with a house, outhouses, yard, garden and pond, was probably situated close to the Queen's Head in the village of Great Stanmore. The Duke agreed to lay out £20 towards the repair of the premises and to allow the elm trees around the pond to be cut down and disposed of by Thomas Wrench. Stuff to repair the railings next to the road and bushes and stakes to make a good hedge around the garden and orchard, and rough timber for future repairs would all be found by the Duke. His own plumber at Canons would repair the pump and gutter and the glass windows were also to be repaired at his Grace's expense. The rent was £10 per annum, clear of all taxes save the Land Tax, and Thomas Wrench had to provide the Duke with a fat capon at Christmas.[22] Several leases refer to giving fat capon or other fowl and these hark back to medieval practice. Instead of a quit rent of fowls, Richard Woods was to carry two loads of coals from London to Canons each year.

## THE END OF THE DUCAL PALACE

Despite the lavish living and extravagance that gave the illusion of boundless wealth, the first Duke was soon short of money, as he speculated in the South Sea Bubble and other precarious ventures. His second wife, Cassandra, died in 1735 and he married thirdly, Lydia, the widow of Sir Thomas Davell, a London merchant, bringing him £40,000. This was not enough, however, to keep his debtors at bay and when he died in 1744, his son, Henry, 2nd Duke of Chandos, was obliged to sell Canons. The house was demolished and pieces were scattered far and wide following a series of sales and auctions in 1747 and 1748. The painted ceilings and window glass from the chapel were reused at Lord Foley's church at Witley Court, Worcestershire. Statues of the first two King Georges found their way to London squares. George I on a horse was until 1873, in Leicester Square and George II is still to be seen in Golden Square. William Hallett, a cabinet-maker of Long Acre, bought the site in 1753 and built himself a more modest house (*ill. 18*), which still stands, with modifications and extensions.

Gainsborough's portrait in the National Gallery, of William Hallett's grandson, William, and his wife, painted about the time of their marriage in 1785, is believed to show them taking a morning stroll in the grounds of Canons. Two years later Canons was sold to Colonel Dennis O'Kelly, owner

*23. The Croft was built at the turn of this century at the southern end of the Manor House grounds. Samuel Wallrock remodelled it in 1930 and incorporated ancient glass and other materials to fit his notion of an old manor house. It is now the Air Commodore's house.*

24.  Samuel Wallrock also renovated the outbuildings of the Manor House, making them into a guest house (seen here) and a ballroom.  The outbuildings have since become the property of St John's church.

25.  The gardens of the Manor House were laid out afresh by Samuel Wallrock.  MOD housing and Tudor Well Close now cover most of them and the northern section became Bernays Gardens in 1948.

*26. The Tudor well which was probably a feature of Samuel Wallrock's gardens has given its name to Tudor Well Close, which was built in 1970.*

of a very famous racehorse, Eclipse. Edward Cutler, grandson of Sir Thomas Plumer, a later owner, remembered Eclipse's skin being stretched on a frame in the stables.[23] The O'Kelly family were in possession until 1812, when Plumer, (1753-1824), Attorney-General and later Master of the Rolls, bought the property and employed Humphry Repton to renovate the grounds. His great-grandson sold the house and park to Dr David Begg in 1860. Maybe the main house needed to be refurbished, for he and his family along with a butler and other servants were living in the North Lodge at the time of the 1861 census. He died in 1868. After his widow's death in 1887 her trustees divided up the estate and auctioned it as nine lots. Morris Jenks bought it all, presumably as a speculation, and sold it on to the Canons Park Estate Company in 1896. The land was to be developed, but Sir Arthur du Cros of the Dunlop Rubber Company bought the mansion in 1906 and had it extended to the designs of Charles E. Mallows. Some of the estate was sold but there were still 150 acres around the house in 1920, when it was offered for sale again. Harrow Urban District Council bought a portion to become the public park which still remains and the North London Collegiate School acquired the mansion and ten acres and moved there in 1929 (*see p128*). Other parts of the estate were developed for housing. (*See pp134-135*).

## THE END OF THE STANMORE LORDSHIP

Although their days of glory were over in Stanmore, the 2nd and 3rd Dukes of Chandos continued as lords of the now united manors. Henceforth, Little Stanmore was subsumed within the manor of Great Stanmore. The third duke, who died in 1789, left no sons and his widow was declared a lunatic in 1793. His daughter's husband, Earl Temple, was created Duke of Buckingham and Chandos in 1813 and he and their son, Richard Plantagenet Temple-Nugent-Brydges-Grenville, continued as lords of the manor in turn, until 1840. The lordship was then sold to the Marquess of Abercorn who lived at Bentley Priory and sold again in 1863 to John Kelk, the next owner of the Priory.[24] The Clutterbucks, who had a brewery on Stanmore Hill were the last family to be lords of the manor of Stanmore. Thomas Clutterbuck had moved to Micklefield Hall, Rickmansworth, by the time that he purchased the manor from John Kelk in 1882. He was succeeded by his son and grandson, who died in 1933 and the last manorial rights were extinguished in 1935.

As to the Manor House of Great Stanmore at the top of Old Church Lane, Richard Plantagenet had sold this to Thomas Otway-Mayne in 1837 while disposing of other manorial property and prerogatives. It continued in use as a private house until it was wantonly demolished in 1930. An earlier historian of Stanmore said that it had no special features to commend it except that it was a good specimen of late sixteenth-century work! The Otway-Maynes lived there during the 1840s and 50s and Mrs Sperling in the late 1860s. Frederick Gordon, who was running Bentley Priory as a hotel at the time, purchased the Manor House and grounds in 1890 and a house called The Croft was built in the southern part of the gardens in 1901. Samuel Wallrock remodelled The Croft 1930-3, giving it a distinctly Tudor appearance with the incorporation of old timbers brought from other places. He renamed it the New Manor House when the old one was demolished. He treated the outbuildings in the same manner and these today are known as Church House and can be approached through Bernays' Memorial Gardens and certainly lend a charming and old-world appearance to the top of Old Church Lane. The New Manor House was bought by the Ministry of Defence in 1940. (*See p138 for further history*).

27.   *The site of St Mary's, the medieval parish church of Great Stanmore, in Old Church Lane.  It was uncovered in 1889 when an accommodation road was being made to go under the new Stanmore & Harrow branch line.*

# The Parish Church of Great Stanmore

## THE MEDIEVAL CHURCH

A medieval parish church dedicated to St Mary stood down Old Church Lane, close to the moated manor house.  It was used until 1632.  Remains were discovered in 1889 when an accommodation road was being made to go under the railway line then being constructed, and again in 1892 when houses were being built in the lane.  They suggested a small fourteenth-century building with fifteenth-century extensions.  Whether the church which is presumed to have been looked after by the priest mentioned in the Domesday Survey was on the same spot or not, is uncertain.  Hugh Braun, archaeologist and a founder member of the Stanmore Historical Society, later examined the rough drawings that had been made of the foundations and thought that the church had been buttressed at the west end because of its proximity to the Stanburn stream and that a new chancel had been built in the fifteenth century, and the nave

extended even further west, closer to the stream at the same time.

There is no record of what happened to the many graves which must surely have been found during the building operations on the site, except for one, the tombstone of Baptist Willoughby, rector from 1563 to 1610.  It is in the garden of Haslemere, no. 44 Old Church Lane.  One monument from the inside of the old building has survived and can be seen in the present church of St John the Evangelist, having in the meantime spent more than 200 years in the intermediate church that is now a ruin.  This colourful and attractive monument commemorates John Burnell, 'merchant of London and Freeman of the Worshipful Company of Clothworkers', who leased the manor of Great Stanmore from c1599, and his wife, Barbara, who continued as lady of the manor after his death in 1605.  Husband and wife are shown kneeling on either side of a *prie dieu*, with their four sons and four daughters kneeling beneath.  The youngest girl holds a skull in her hands and her next sister has a skull on the ground beside her.  The second youngest boy sits gazing outwards with a grin on his face and holding a skull on his lap.  The three children with the symbols of mortality are thought to have died young, the boy probably being

28. *The gravestone of Baptist Willoughby, rector from 1563 to 1610, in the garden of Haslemere, 44 Old Church Lane.*

29. *The Burnell monument erected to the memory of John Burnell of the Clothworkers' Company after his death in 1605, was moved to the new church in 1632 and finally to the present St John's. One of the sons sits gazing outwards, rather than in an attitude of prayer, perhaps suggesting that he was mentally retarded.*

mentally retarded. Barbara Burnell left two shillings per year to the parish clerk to keep the family monument 'clean without dust' when she died in 1632, a sum which he was still receiving in 1933. It has been restored by the Clothworkers' Company on several occasions.

## A NEW BRICK CHURCH

During the rectorship of Henry Raynsford (1618-49) a new church was erected on the north side of Colliers Lane, opposite the new manor house and near to what was becoming the centre of the village of Great Stanmore. The manor house certainly came first, because John Burnell repaired the house on the new site during his lordship. The reason for moving the church is not clear, but Richard Newcourt in his *Repertorium ecclesiasticum parochiale Londinense* of 1710 wrote 'The church which formerly belonged to this parish being too remote from it and very ruinous was by Licence frrom the Bishop of London totally demolished and a very fair new church built in a more convenient position'. So, the old building may have

been in a bad state as well as having been left standing in an isolated position among fields. Nothing is really known about its fate. Perhaps it was left to fall into decay and was used as a quarry for useful building materials, but it does not seem to have been completely demolished, because the tower appears faintly in the distance in three views of the new brick church taken from the north east, dated 1791, 1799 and one undated but slightly later.

The new church was paid for by Sir John Wolstenholme and the land was given by Sir Thomas Lake, Mr Burnell (son of the John Burnell mentioned above), and a Mr Robinson. Wolstenholme (1562-1639) was the second son of a John Wolstenholme who had come to London from the north of England about the middle of the sixteenth century, obtained a post in the Customs and acquired Goodalls and other properties in Stanmore: he was buried at the old church in 1603.

*30. The new church of 1632 dedicated to St John, was situated near to the new manor house at the top of Old Church Lane and the centre of population. St Mary's was said to have been totally demolished, but a distant church tower, which appears to be that of the old church, can be discerned in this print of 1799.*

His son was a Merchant Adventurer and was knighted in 1617. He was involved in the setting up of the East India Company in 1600 and was on the council of the Virginia Company in 1609. Thereafter he rose in the ranks of the Company, being appointed Commissioner for the Plantation of Virginia in 1631. He encouraged maritime exploration and financed two expeditions to find the north-west passage. The first in 1610 was led by Henry Hudson and the second in 1615 by William Baffin. Cape Wolstenholme at the entrance to Hudson's Bay, Wolstenholme Sound and Wolstenholme Island, all in Canada, were named after him and the first English settlers to reach the James River in Virginia in 1618 called their settlement Wolstenholme Town. The town was deserted after a massacre by Indians in 1662 and only rediscovered and excavated in 1970.

## A PREACHING BOX

Sir John was considered one of the wealthiest London merchants and could have afforded a lavishly decorated church, but his tastes evidently ran to simplicity in religious matters. The church was built of brick in English Bond and had a Portland stone south porch designed by Nicholas

Stone (1586-1647), master mason to James I and Charles I. It was a plain, simple church, consisting of a nave, but no choir or chancel and the interior was filled with high-backed pews and galleries. The font, decorated with the Wolstenholme coat-of-arms, (now in the present church), is also the work of Stone. The church was consecrated by William Laud, Bishop of London on 17 July 1632 and dedicated to St John, a change from the medieval dedication, perhaps in honour of Wolstenholme himself. Laud noted in his diary that the church was built by 'Sir Jo. Walstenham' and this simple statement was twisted and used against him at his trial for high treason in 1644, when he was accused of papistical practices in consecrating private chapels, 'the chapel of Sir John Worsterham's building' being cited. He replied that it was not a chapel, but a true parish church.

Watercolours and other pictures of the late eighteenth and early nineteenth century show the brick church with iron angle ties holding the walls in place and a heavy growth of ivy, cut back from time to time, but threatening to overwhelm the structure. By the 1840s the building was in need of extensive repair and somewhat overcrowded on Sunday mornings – by the middle of the cen-

31. *St John's drawn on 19 September 1807 by William Ellis, showing the west end and tower with a luxuriant growth of ivy. The rectory of 1721, designed by Edward Shepherd, is on the right.*

32. *The preaching box – this lithograph by J.C. Oldmeadow of Bushey, showing the interior of St John's, dates from c1840. Beside the altar stands the four-poster bed monument of Sir John Wolstenholme, grandson of the founder, who died in 1669.*

*33.   Death mask of Sir John Wolstenholme who died in 1639.  The mask was made when his coffin was opened in 1870.*

*34.   Monument by Nicholas Stone to Sir John Wolstenholme.*

*35.   The 4th Earl of Aberdeen laying the foundation stone of Great Stanmore's present parish church on 14 March 1849.  Queen Adelaide, who was living at Bentley Priory, was present.  The site was a field given by Lt Col. Hamilton Tovey-Tennant, west of the 1632 church.  On this lithograph by J.C. Oldmeadow, the rectory gates can be seen on the right across the present Rectory Lane.  The houses in view are probably Pynnacles on the left and the Manor House on the right.*

tury 400-450 people were attending services. Arthur Chauvel, the minister, had been at Stanmore since 1788 and must have been growing old, which may account for some of the disrepair and perhaps an unwillingness to countenance change.  The churchwardens sent out a circular dated 27 September 1844, requesting all parishioners to attend a Vestry meeting on the following Monday to discuss proposed alterations;[1] later a survey of the building was made.

## THE NEW CHURCH OF ST JOHN THE EVANGELIST

On the 22 June 1848 the Bishop of London wrote to the new, young rector, the Hon. Douglas Gordon, son of the 4th Earl of Aberdeen (patron of the living), urging the building of a new church because it was not possible to provide better accommodation in the existing building. No doubt changing views in the church at large, emanating from the burgeoning Oxford Movement, influenced the ideas of the patron and leading parishioners about the style of church architecture and the rituals of worship. Lt Col. Tovey-Tennent who lived at Pynnacles at the corner of Green Lane, offered a piece of land adjoining the churchyard, as a site and the Earl of Aberdeen gave his full consent for the erection of a new church in August 1848.[2] A vestry meeting, held on 17 October 1848, heard a letter from Henry Clutton, architect of Whitehall Place, explaining why the old church could not be extended, and took an unanimous decision to erect a new building. Queen Adelaide, who was spending the last months of her life at Bentley Priory, attended the laying of the foundation stone by the Earl of Aberdeen on 14 March 1849. It was her last public appearance. A handsome building in Decorated style was designed by Clutton and built by George Myers, and consecrated on 17 July 1850, 218 years to the day after Laud had consecrated its forerunner. Lord Aberdeen and his son had contributed £3000 towards the cost of £7855, and another £3000 was raised by a church rate; the balance came from subscriptions.

The original plan was to demolish the brick church as soon as the new one was in operation. It may have been for this reason that the monuments of the Burnell family, Sir John Wolstenholme, the founder, and that of his grandson, another Sir John, were moved to the new church. In 1870 the Revd Leopold Bernays opened the Wolstenholme tomb in the presence of a Doctor Rogers and found the first Sir John, who had died in 1639, in such a wonderful state of preservation that it was possible to make a death mask. There is a clear likeness between the mask, which is kept at the church, and the effigy on the tomb. Although the first Sir John's monument, by Nicholas Stone, is very fine, the other is much more spectacular, being in the form of a four-poster bed in white marble, on which the young man reclines with his wife beside him, leaning over and wiping his brow with a lace handkerchief. Two children lie at the side of the bed. The second Sir John died in 1669. Owing to its size this bed/monument is housed in the tower out of sight.

*36. St John the Evangelist, designed by Henry Clutton of Whitehall Place, newly built in 1850.*

*37. The Marquess of Aberdeen unveiling a plaque in honour of the 4th Earl of Aberdeen, whose coffin was discovered during the consolidation of the ruined church 1991-2. The ceremony was attended by Dr David Hope, Bishop of London, and was held on 17 July 1992, exactly 360 years after Archbishop Laud consecrated the church.*

## THE RUIN

Views on the architectural merits of the brick church varied. S.L. Bernays thought it was an extraordinarily ugly building inside, but J. Taverner-Perry, in *Old Memorials of Middlesex*, believed it to be a really noble building which ought never to have been allowed to become disused, and contrasted it favourably with the new St John's, which he considered 'a somewhat imposing and pretentious fabric, an imitation of fourteenth century work'. Popular affection for the older church building seems to have forced the church authorities to change their plans about demolition and after the roof had been removed by a local contractor it was left to become a romantic, ivy-covered ruin, gently mouldering away, attracting artists and the curious antiquarian. Vandals in the 1970s did much damage to the structure, and particularly to the tombs left within the walls. The whole place became unsafe and was labelled 'Dangerous structure - keep out'. The Historic Buildings Committee of the London & Middlesex Archaeological Society lobbied the Council for the Care of Churches and English Heritage, until the ruin was eventually consolidated and made safe in 1991. The Abercorn vault was unearthed during the work and the coffin of Lord Aberdeen was discovered in it.

## PATRONS AND RECTORS
### Patrons
The Abbey of St Albans was in possession of the church until the dissolution of the monasteries and normally appointed a rector to care for the souls of the parishioners. After 1539 the right of presentation to the living was taken over by the Crown for a time and then went with the ownership of the manor until the death of James, 1st Duke of Chandos. He left the patronage to trustees, who sold it to Andrew Drummond of Stanmore Park. The Abercorn family, into which Lord Aberdeen married, took it over by purchase during their years at Bentley Priory. The Revd Leopold John Bernays bought the patronage from the Earl of Aberdeen and presented R.G. Gorton in 1857, becoming rector himself in 1860. The patronage has been in the hands of the Bernays trustees ever since. Richard Bernays is patron in 1998.

### The Rectory
It is not clear where the rectors lived until 1721, when the 1st Duke of Chandos assisted George Hudson to build a new rectory, designed by the architect Edward Shepherd, close to the church. It can be seen in the background on several pictures of the brick church, a Georgian house with

*38. The garden front of the 1721 rectory with its ornamental lake.*

a pedimented gable, overlooking a small lake. It was enlarged in 1850 by the addition of a wing, but was inevitably considered too large by the middle of the twentieth century. It was divided into separate dwellings in 1949 and demolished in 1960. The present rectory is very near to the old site.

## The Glebe land

The glebe was the land allocated to the incumbent of a parish for his maintenance. In addition he received the tithes from parishioners. At one time tithes in kind were paid, but these were commuted to money payments over the centuries. When tithes were suppressed in Stanmore in 1838, the rector was granted £444 a year in lieu. The glebe land in Great Stanmore amounted to about sixty acres in 1086. In medieval times it would have been scattered about the common fields in the form of selions (strips) of about three quarters of an acre each. By the seventeenth century it had been reduced to 32 acres, some known as Parsonage Field. The glebe ran close to Stanmore Park, home of the Drummond family, and James Dalton, rector 1781-88, under the terms of a private act of parliament, exchanged 12 acres 2 roods 16 perches

*39. The tithe barn near the rectory in Old Church Lane. Part of it probably dates from the sixteenth century, but the Duke of Chandos gave materials to rebuild it in 1730. About 1930 it was converted into three houses, Tithe Barn, Stanburn House and Old Church House by Mr F. Cane.*

*40. Some of the outbuildings of the Manor House were taken over by the church after Samuel Wallrock left the new Manor House. They are used as a church room and there are two cottages, one the home of the caretaker.*

of land, including the old churchyard of the medieval church, with George Drummond, receiving 19 acres 3 roods 4 perches of the Great and Little Meadows, which had formerly been known as the Haw Meadows.[3] In later years the glebe was sold off for building. Glebe Road, the Bernays Institute and the Glebe council estate are all built on glebeland.

### Rectors

Three rectors were appointed in 1349, which might have led one to suppose that the Black Death was taking its toll in Stanmore, had it been the previous year. Little is known of the religious views of the people during the Reformation. William Creeting, who was appointed in 1527, survived the changes of Henry VIII's reign, but was replaced at the beginning of Edward VI's reign by Alfonsus de Salignas who sounds Spanish and was appointed by Pedro de Gamboa. He seems to have been an absentee who paid a substitute priest for an unknown length of time, as there is a gap in the records until Baptist Willoughby arrived in 1563, well into Elizabeth's reign, when the upheavals of the Reformation had died down. There is little evidence of opposition to the religious changes at Stanmore. Only one recusant is recorded, Thomas

Norwood, member of a prominent landowning family.

Baptist Willoughby was probably 31 years old when he became rector and had graduated from Brasenose College, Oxford in 1557. He stayed until his death in 1610. He was a preacher of some renown, being nominated to deliver seven of fifteen sermons endowed by Robert Hilson, a relative by marriage of the Burnell family. Mr Hilson had heard him in the 'very large and fair gallery in the ould church belonging to Stanmore Magna. Mr Willoughby had built the gallery at his own charge and expense'. There may have been a relationship with the Burnells because John Burnell's will (proved 1605) refers to a Widow Willoughby of Dover, which was where the Burnells came from, and to Baptist Willoughby in the next clause. He was to have a mourning gown.

The Wolstenholmes were also friends of Mr Willoughby. When he died he left 'a pretty diall' to Mistress John Wolstenholme and 'an ell of fyne cloth be yt holland or cambricke which I have in my deske' to Henry Wolstenholme's wife. Their husbands were to have twenty shillings in gold each to make rings to be worn in remembrance of him. He expressed a wish to be buried as near to their father, his old friend John Wolstenholme, as conveniently might be.

*41. Stanmore Free Church near Elm Park Tennis Club.*

The next period of religious strife was during the Civil War and Commonwealth, when there was an attempt to rid the church of Anglican clergymen and the Prayer Book. Matthew Playford was made rector in 1649 upon the probably enforced resignation of Henry Rainsford, and Samuel Slantcliffe came in 1658. He was ejected in 1662, two years after the restoration of Charles II. The parish registers for the years 1645 to 1654 were very sketchily kept, suggesting that the clergy were conforming to puritanical edicts and not keeping ecclesiastical registers. However, both Rainsford and Slantcliffe recorded the births and baptisms of their own children in the old register book that runs from 1599-1702 and the burials of the more prominent members of the congregation. The single entry for the year 1649 relates to Elizabeth Burnell widow and late wife of Mr William Burnell of this parish[4].

Two Victorian rectors were Bernays. Leopold John Bernays, rector 1860-83, was chairman of the Stanmore Gas Company and took an interest in the Colne Valley Water Company. He gave the Bernays Memorial Institute which still stands in the centre of Stanmore, in memory of his son, Ernest, who was drowned on holiday. Another of his sons, S.F.L. Bernays, was rector from 1898-1924. He took an interest in the documents of the church, and he recorded the registers then in existence in an article in the *Home Counties Magazine*, Vol III, 1901 'as an incentive to my successors to preserve them.' About the time that he became rector, a Mission Hut was built at Little Common adjoining the fire engine shack near the Spring Pond.

## OTHER CHURCHES [5]

Mr Bernays mentioned in a sermon in 1912 that there had never been a chapel in the whole history of the village, but in fact there had been independent meeting houses from time to time, although the exact position of the earlier ones are unknown. The longest lasting was licensed from 1689-1719 and there were others in 1826 and 1833. The Primitive Methodists had a preaching room from 1882, but had ceased by 1896, before Mr Bernays was rector.

There was a Baptist meeting room in Church Road in 1889, but the present Baptist Church in Abercorn Road dates from 1935 when suburban housing was spreading. It is affiliated to the Baptist Union. It arose from meetings organised by the builder, Henry J. Clare, for his workmen and held in an old barn in Old Church Lane. Another Baptist group also used the barn and opened a chapel in Marsh Lane in 1937, being a member of the Fellowship of Independent Evangelical Churches.

Stanmore Free Church near Elm Park Tennis Club was established in 1936 after several years of meetings in private houses.

## THE PARISH CLERK

At the court[6] held on the Tuesday after the Epiphany 1508, the field called Staples at the southern end of the parish was granted to a group of four men who were to act as trustees and yearly find a parish clerk for the parish church of Stanmore. Four honest men of the town of Stanmore were always to be appointed trustees of the land. The parish clerk had the benefit of the land for which he was to pay one penny at Easter. In return he was to attend the manor courts when a tenant had died, presumably to announce their deaths to the homage.

The first four 'honest men' had an interest in the land: John Warner, described as smith and yeoman, Roger Edlyn, yeoman, Robert Person, yeoman and Robert Goldhurst, husbandman. However, John Warner produced a son who became the Warden of All Souls College in 1536 and the first Regius Professor of Medicine at Oxford in 1546. He was a clergyman as well as a doctor and became Dean of Winchester. He was buried at Stanmore.

Clerk's Staples, as the field came to be known, was usually rented at between £10 and £12 per annum and so continued until the 1920s when a small portion was sold to Hendon Rural District Council for the site of an Isolation Hospital. The rest of the field was developed after the opening of the Metropolitan Line in 1932.

# St Lawrence's, Little Stanmore

## THE EARLY CHURCH

Roger de Rames, grandson of the Domesday owner, gave a church in Little Stanmore to St Bartholomew's Priory, Smithfield, sometime after 1130.[1] It was dedicated to St Lawrence. Nothing is known of the building except that it was probably whitewashed on the outside, as the name Whitchurch became attached to the church and the surrounding area. Towards the end of the fifteenth century the church seems to have had a new tower built on the old foundations and it is that which today is the sole surviving part of the early church. St Bartholomew's Priory owned the church and appointed priests to serve it, until the Reformation. Unfortunately a list of incumbents has not survived and only a few names are known.

During the religious troubles of the Reformation, the priest, Richard Davy, who was said to be a former Carthusian, was denounced by clergy at Hendon and Kingsbury for objecting to removing statues from his church.[2] Had he fled to Stanmore after the

martyrdom of his fellow Carthusians at the London Charterhouse in 1535? Whatever the priest's views the statues went and the people of Little Stanmore conformed to the new order. A certificate of goods of the church of Stanmore the Less,[3] dated 3 August 1552, gives some idea of the alterations made to the furnishings and interior to comply with the new religious rituals imposed by Edward VI. Edward Downer, a joiner of Edgware, set up the pulpit in the middle of the church according to the king's injunctions and mended the seats. A 'table to minister the communyon' was bought for 6s 0d and a new bible cost 13s 0d. The churchwardens, Gabriel Pawlyn and John Homes, recouped some of the expenses by selling the now redundant religious objects, such as a veil cloth that used to cover the statues during Lent. A pyx cloth was worth four shillings, but the old, ragged altar cloth that was sold with it brought in only four pence. A Dutchman dwelling in St Martin's, London, gave 4s 4d for a processional cross of copper and gilt and a staff. All the old Latin books were delivered to the Bishop's officers at Westminster and a book by Erasmus was purchased with money obtained by the sale of two censors and a boat used for incense.

The tower had a battlemented top and steeple, according to an item for repairs in the certificate. Lead had been blown off the steeple, presumably in

*42. St Lawrence Whitchurch in 1808. This engraving of a drawing by Ellis shows the medieval tower at the west end of the Duke of Chandos's church. It is built of red brick and flint rubble, rendered with cement.*

43. *This picture shows the body of the church built in the main by John James 1714-16. Several wooden graveboards can be seen, a common feature of graveyards in Middlesex where local stone was not available. The boards run the length of the grave and details of the deceased were inscribed on them by signwriters.*

the previous winter. The cost of laying of the lead and repair of the battlements was 3s 4d and the tiles, ridge tiles, nails, lime and sand amounted to 12s 2d. The Edgware joiner's bill for 8s 3d covered the repair of 'the Church house' as well as the moving of the pulpit and repair of seats. This is an interesting and solitary reference to a church house. Many parishes had such places, similar to a modern church hall, and in other Middlesex parishes like Northolt and Ruislip they were subsequently used to house the poor. It is possible that Lady Lake's almshouses replaced the one in Little Stanmore.

After the Reformation, St Lawrence's was held by succeeding lords of the manor: Hugh Losse, the Lake family and the Dukes of Chandos. As we have seen (p17), James Brydges (later 1st Duke of Chandos) paid for a splendid baroque place of worship to be built for the parish, at the same time as he was creating his palatial Canons. The new church was built onto the existing tower between 1714-16 and still stands today.

## BAROQUE SPLENDOUR

Stepping into St Lawrence's is like entering an intimate theatre. The altar stands beneath an arch, flanked by wooden columns with Corinthian capitals, carved by Grinling Gibbons and above it, as if on a stage, rises the organ upon which Handel sometimes played. Paintings by Belluci, of the *Nativity* and the *Descent from the cross* on either side of the altar and Verrio's *Sermon on the Mount* and *Moses receiving the ten commandments* beside the organ, form a backdrop. Laguerre's *Adoration of Jehovah* covers the ceiling above the altar and a sky scene conveys the impression of a suitable 'heaven' above the organ. A gilded wooden 'curtain' is suspended from the 'proscenium' arch. The theatrical effect continues at the back of the church, where shallow stairs lead to the Chandos family box, in a central position looking straight down the nave to the altar/stage. His box is replete with the comfort of a fireplace and decorated with a copy of Raphael's *Transfiguration* on the ceiling. To one side another box housed his bodyguard of ex-soldiers and on the other on rather uncomfortable, narrow wooden benches, sat his household. Grisaille paintings by Francesco Sleter, of Faith, Hope and Charity and the gospel writers filling the walls of the nave and the miracles of Christ by Laguerre, in sepia on the ceiling, provide a sober and more tranquil centre to the church between the exuberant colour and gilding at both ends. The visitor could be forgiven for believing himself far from Middlesex, having wandered into a Bavarian church interior.

John James, the architect who designed the church and the artists who worked there were also employed at Canons. The paintings and plaster work were in a bad state by 1970 and only saved by a national appeal. The paintings have recently been cleaned and restored.

## THE MAUSOLEUM

The church was first built with a room on the north-east side meant to house the Chandos family monuments, but the 1st Duke felt that more space was needed for a suitable memorial, after his second wife, Cassandra, died in 1735, so James Gibbs added

*45. The theatrical east end of St Lawrence's earlier this century. The screen, which has since been removed, obscures the view of the organ on which Handel sometimes played. Grinling Gibbons almost certainly carved the wooden columns and capitals.*

*44. The Duke of Chandos's box, complete with fireplace, dominates the west end of the church. His bodyguard and servants sat in the smaller boxes on either side. A copy of Raphael's* Transfiguration *decorates the ceiling.*

46.  The font at Whitchurch.

47.  The monument to the 1st Duke of Chandos, thought
to be by Grinling Gibbons, in the mausoleum attached to
the church.  Mary Lake (d.1712), his first wife, kneels on
his right and Cassandra (d. 1735), his second wife, on
his left.

48.  18th century coffins beneath the mausoleum.  The
double coffin contains the remains of a mother and
daughter who died many years apart.  There are separate
inner coffins.

the mausoleum.  It is divided from the original
monument room, now known as the antechamber,
by wrought iron gates.  A monument thought to be
by Grinling Gibbons, showing the 1st Duke in Roman dress, standing in a central position, with Mary
Lake, his first wife, kneeling on his right and
Cassandra kneeling on his left, dominates the room.
The family vault lies underneath.  Gaetano Brunetti
who probably helped Sleter with the grisaille paintings in the nave, decorated the walls and ceiling
with *trompe l'oeil* figures and columns.

## PATRONS AND INCUMBENTS
Puritanical feeling and a desire for good sermons
increased in the seventeenth century.  Possibly Lady
Lake, the patron of the parish, disagreed with the
religious views of the incumbent in 1638, as she
threatened him with destitution by removing him
from his house beside the church, but she was ordered to leave him undisturbed.  The survey of
church livings in Middlesex made in 1649 says: 'We
have one ecclesiastical benefice with the cure of souls
and Lancelot Lake Esq, is the impropriator of the
same and we conceive tithes and profits thereof to
be worth about fifty pounds per annum and one Mr
Nicholas Holland is our constant preaching minister placed with us by the said Mr Lake of whom he
received £40 per annum as his salary.  And all our
parishioners may conveniently come to our parish
church to attend the worship and service of God'.

*49. John Theophilus Desaguiliers (1683-1744), first rector of the new church at Little Stanmore.*

*50. A pleasant rural scene in Whitchurch Lane in 1892.*

James Brydges appointed John Theophilus Desaguiliers (1683-1744) to St Lawrence's in 1714, perhaps because he wanted this talented man's advice on his waterworks in the gardens at Canons. Desaguiliers had been born in La Rochelle and brought to England by his Huguenot parents. He was a natural philosopher who published works on physics, astronomy and mechanics and is best remembered for having invented the planetarium, an early model of the planetary system. Complaints were made that he neglected his parishioners for the more beguiling and intellectually stimulating work at Canons, actually leaving a corpse in the church for three days on one occasion because he could not spare the time to bury it.[4]

The Revd Benjamin John Armstrong, who was at Whitchurch from 1844-50, kept a diary[5] for most of his life, but it has very few entries for the years at Stanmore. Perhaps he was too busy filling the church, for he comments that when he arrived only 150 parishioners attended, a figure which he managed to double in his six year incumbency. The problem with St Lawrence's was that most of the houses in the parish were on the west side of Edgware village and it was just as easy for the inhabitants to worship at St Margaret's, the parish church of Edgware. The neighbouring church had long encroached upon Little Stanmore. In the 1649 survey of church livings the Edgware entry runs:

'Little Stanmore lying near to us may fitly be united to us and made one parish'. Mr Armstrong found the bulk of the congregation 'decidedly puritan', whereas he was a moderate Tractarian (early Oxford Movement). He writes 'I have boys', girls' and Sunday schools at the former of which I lecture for an hour on Tuesdays and Fridays; also a coal and bread charity, clothing club, parochial library, field garden allotments; and I visit every family certainly four times a year'.

This obvious zeal and capacity for hard work could not have been expected from the earlier entries in his diary which describe one sporting event after another – hunts with the Queen's Stag Hounds, the Royal and Old Berkeley, attendance at Pinner Races and partridge shooting. In 1840, the year he was ordained, he attended a coursing meeting at Osterley on the 7th March; had 'a splendid run ' with Mr Anderson's stag hounds on the 10th, going from Hayes to Rickmansworth without a check; and on the 14th, he writes 'I met the Queen's in the same neighbourhood and had an hour and 35 minutes over the grass without a check; the deer was taken at Stanmore'. He published a history of the church and parish in 1849 and moved to East Dereham, Norfolk the following year.

There were disputes over the patronage of the church early in the nineteenth century and it passed from hand to hand until 1929 when it was taken over by the Bishop of London.

### THE PARSONAGE

Very little is known about the house of the early incumbents, except that it was near the church. A new rectory was built on the east side of the church in 1852, designed by Anthony Salvin. This survived until 1967 when it was cleared to make way for St Lawrence Close, where the present smaller vicarage stands and a church hall.

### OTHER CHURCHES WITHIN THE OLD PARISH

There was no recorded outcry against the religious changes of the Reformation and only Richard Gill in 1611 and Joan Brickhill and Alice Rumball between 1624-35, were fined as recusants from Little Stanmore. There were no further signs of Roman Catholicism in the parish until the Dominican convent and school of St Thomas Aquinas opened in Marsh Lane in the mid-1930s. This centre formed the basis of a Catholic mission and the parish of St William of York was founded in 1938, with masses open to the public being said at the convent chapel on weekdays and in the school on Sundays. A new church was built in Du Cros Drive in 1960.

An independent chapel opened in Edgware High Street near the Mason's Arms in 1834, though the

*51. Little Stanmore Rectory designed by Anthony Salvin 1852.*

*52. This early 18th-century gravestone in St Lawrence's, commemorating members of the Cook and Waterfall families, is one of several in the churchyard carved with rather chilling memento mori.*

independents had been worshipping in the area since at least 1801. The chapel was closed between 1881and 1893, then was in use until 1937, when a new chapel was built in Grove Road, Edgware. The Baptist church in Camrose Avenue opened in 1935, services having been held in a tent since the previous year.

The synagogue in London Road was built in 1951 and the adjoining community centre in 1963.

# Life in early rural Stanmore

## THE COMMON FIELDS

The Domesday Survey of 1086 suggests that a considerable portion of the two Stanmores was either plough land or former arable that could be brought back into cultivation again if economic conditions were right. It is reasonable to suppose that in medieval times both manors had common fields that were subdivided by ditches into stadia, which were in turn cut up into selions or strips of land about ∫ acre in size. The villeins normally had numbers of selions scattered around the common fields making up their holdings, which were attached to a messuage (dwelling house) or tenement. The holdings were usually fractions of a hide (c120 acres), the quarter hide, known as a virgate (c30 acres) being a common peasant tenement. Usually the houses had closes of land around them used as gardens, orchards and for grazing. Some cottages simply had the small enclosures and no land in the common fields.

There is scant reference to common arable fields in Little Stanmore, but they must have existed as 'pasture on the several and common fields for 140 sheep' is mentioned in records belonging to St Bartholomew's in 1306.[1]

Great Stanmore had common arable fields as late as the nineteenth century. Thomas Milne's land use map of 1800 shows them coloured brown and lying well south of the moated manor site down Old Church Lane, extending to the boundary with Kenton on the south and to the lands of Little Stanmore on the east. They probably stretched further north and west at an earlier period. Hugh Braun's conjectural map[2] (*ill. 53*) of medieval Great Stanmore shows Hither Field reaching from the manor site as far north as Colliers Lane and Church Road; Further Field running up from Kenton Fields; and Middle Field in between. Alternative names, the Wheatfield, Beanfield and Fallowfield, reflecting the crops grown and the practice of leaving land fallow every third year, occur in sixteenth-century wills. Roger Evelyn, whose will was proved in 1508, left his two sons a breadth of land lying in the fallow field which was to be sown that year with wheat, at his wife's cost.[3]

All the fields extended to the boundary with Harrow Weald. Court rolls show that tenants with lands bordering Harrow Weald and Kenton were responsible for maintaining hedges and ditches

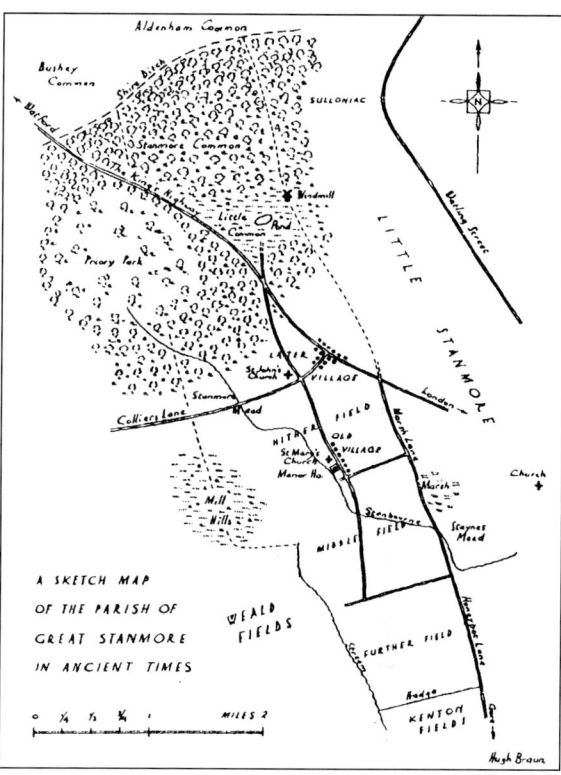

53. *Conjectural map of Great Stanmore in ancient times by Hugh Braun. He places the windmill on the boundary of the two manors, roughly in what later became the grounds of The Grove.*

between the manors and were frequently penalised for failing to do so.[4] In October 1578 it was found that all the tenants had diligently observed the order except John Warren who happened to have land in Harrow Weald as well as Stanmore and who had ignored complaints made against him at the manor court for several years past. He had eventually submitted himself to the lord and steward of the manor saying that he was content that Bernard Randall, his tenant, should make the ditch and hedge. Thereupon Randall hired William Aylward to do the work, but John Warren's temper was apparently so well known that William refused to start until John had personally given his licence and assent and went round to his house to obtain it. The ditch was made and planted and grew for two years, then was levelled and broken down again. Therefore John Warren was fined 40 shillings and ordered to reinstate the work under pain of paying ten shillings for every perch (5½ yards, approximately 5 metres) not made or planted. His land extended for 8 or 9 perches. He was also fined for failing to close gaps in the Middle Field.

The common field land left in 1800 appears to be mainly the former Further Field. The other two fields had been enclosed piecemeal and become meadow or park land sometime after 1735, when land in all three fields was attached to Harry Bunn's Farm, which was being leased by the Duke of Chandos to Samuel Ward.[5] Incidentally Mr Ward had to pay £41 5s per annum rent, plus two fat capons on 1st January and two guineas in gold on the marriage of the eldest son of the Duke. Ancient rents had often included fowl or eggs and the payment to help the lord defray the wedding expenses of his eldest son, harks back to the feudal dues payable to the king or his tenants-in-chief in medieval times.

The Great Stanmore Lands to Enclose Act was passed in 1813 to deal with the remaining 216 acres of common field. The land was already in the hands of a mere six landowners and the Act was only necessary because 'small parcels of land lie intermixed and disposed and inconveniently situated, and it would be an advantage to such proprietors if the same were divided and allotted among them according to their rights and interests inclosed but such purpose cannot be effected without the aid and authority of Parliament'.

Tenants who had land in the common fields had grazing rights over the fallow field and the other fields after harvest. In 1578 the stint was three sheep for every acre of arable and five sheep for every acre of pasture. Those who put out more than their stint were charged five shillings per sheep.

## CUSTOMARY WORKS

The manors had demesne land – land retained by the lord of the manor – partially enclosed and partially in the common fields. In the Middle Ages the villeins, who were tied to the manor, could be required to work on the demesne for a number of days each week, performing the so-called customary services. Everyone within the manor, even freemen who did not have to perform the week works, laboured on the demesne at busy times like harrowing, haymaking and reaping, usually receiving food for their maintenance during the day and some kind of harvest supper at the

*54. Brockley Hill Farm in Little Stanmore. The 17th-century house is awaiting restoration in 1998. Prior to 1808 this farm was included with Brockley Hill House on the Edgware side of Brockley Hill.*

end. These were called boondays. The better off villeins did not necessarily work themselves, but provided men. The works were in addition to annual rents. No documents survive explaining the exact conditions in Great Stanmore. The sister manor is better recorded. By 1276-7 some labour services had already been commuted to money payments at Little Stanmore,[6] a process that was becoming common in Middlesex at the time as evidenced by the mid-thirteenth century customal of Ruislip. In Stanmore William Wygeburn's works were valued at 8d in addition to his rent of 1s 7d. Commutation accelerated after the Black Death when labour was scarce and by the fifteenth century villeins usually paid a quit rent to be free of all services and the title to their property was a copy of the entry in the court rolls recording their admission to it. They became known as copyholders.

A 1306 rental shows that the tenants of St Bartholomew's Priory performed customary works. The manor house at Canons was surrounded by a close of grassland and had a demesne of 156 acres of arable. There were seven free tenants. Two of them, John Pers and William Pipard, were to come to the great autumn boonday, each bringing two men, and to the lord's boonday, with one man each and they had to see that the men's work was well done. John and William were allowed three meals in the day; bread, beer and cheese at breakfast; bread, beer, broth and a meat and a cheese course at none (literally the ninth hour) and whatever the other reapers were having at vespers (evening).

The villeins were required to work for more days and received less food than the free tenants. They had to weed for two half days without food being provided or two whole days if the lord provided food; similarly lift the hay for two days and harrow for two days. On the two boondays of the lord they had to find two men and only one of them was to have one meal of bread, broth, a main course and cheese. They had to find one man for the great autumn boonday and have two repasts, the evening meal consisting of bread, beer, broth, a main course, milk pudding and cheese. The bread at that meal was to be entirely made of wheat. Some of the villein dwellings were shared and the works were divided between the tenants. The men who worked for the villeins were the descendants of the Domesday Book cottars and their names are unknown to us.

### LITTLE STANMORE IN 1306[7]
The holdings of the sixteen villeins were mostly very small, several under five acres. William Brunnote had the most land: one messuage with

55. *Most of the houses in Little Stanmore from medieval times were probably along Watling Street, the old Roman road. Many of the old buildings there have been lost to developers, but in this section of the street, nos. 95-101 have survived. The timber-framed building with the gable was once the Sawyers' Arms.*

*56.  Another survival in Watling Street, despite being threatened with demolition in 1974, is this shop next to the Masons' Arms.*

nine acres; part of John in le Hale's dwelling and 16 acres of land, three acres of meadow and one acre of pasture as well.  Most of the arable was in the hands of the freemen.  John Barnville had a hide of land and William de la Grave and William Pipard shared one and a half hides, which had formed a separate enclosed estate in the previous century.  The arable land of that estate was near Brockholes, suggesting Brockley Hill.

The population appears to have more than doubled since Domesday for 27 different names appear in the rental as opposed to twelve in 1086.

The field names mentioned were Brockholes, Hountemusfeld and Horscroft and one messuage was called Undemslond.  There is reference to Grenelane (not the present Green Lane which is in Great Stanmore), Umfreyslane and the road to Watford, which crossed Little Stanmore south of the present London Road.  It is difficult from these odd references to work out where the arable fields lay, except for Brockholes.

### Pasture and Woodland

The cows and oxen had their own 54 acres of pasture at Lugpyt and Pyrifeld, while the heifers were pastured separately on 113 acres at Grimesdich and hard by the mill.  The sheep had the common fields after harvest and when one was lying fallow.  The reference to Grimsditch in Little Stanmore is interesting, as it must have been clearly defined and was presumably the section running through the present Pear Wood.  The mill was a windmill, so likely to have been on the hill, where it would catch the breezes.  Braun has placed it somewhere near Wood Lane near the boundary with Great Stanmore on his map.  The name Lugpyt carries on in modified form to the Tithe Award map of 1839 and was north of Whitchurch Lane, near the marsh.  The $56\frac{1}{2}$ acres of woodland were almost certainly the present Pear Wood and were probably composed of oak and coppiced hornbeam, as the underwood (the coppice) was valued at 13s $1\frac{1}{2}$d.

57. *This aerial photograph, taken before 1932, shows several of the former head tenements.  On the right of the picture Dennis Lane runs down to the junction of the Broadway and London Road and Marsh Lane runs from that junction to the bottom of the picture.  On the corner of the Broadway and Dennis Lane stands Fiddles.  Opposite on the corner of Marsh Lane is Pathgate.  Further west along the Broadway the house with the bow front is Montagues (in its 18th-century form).  Opposite on the north side of the Broadway near the junction with Stanmore Hill is Buckingham Cottage, which may have been Mackrells.  Only Pathgate survives.*

## GREAT STANMORE IN THE 1580s[8]

A survey of the manor of Great Stanmore was made in 1588, but it is difficult to relate some of the messuages and tenements named to modern Stanmore.  There were five buildings in the hands of freeholders:

Hugh Jones's tenement, sometime Smiths;

Roger Saunton's house with Collver Croft;

Robert Mosse's great house called the Shread Mill and the Round House built of brick;

Warner Norwood's Harries for which the quit-rent due at midsummer was 'one red rose if it be demanded'.

A house of brick must have been of recent build in 1588, otherwise it would have been of timber frame construction.  The Round House was by the coney warren and sometimes used as a lodge.  Was it circular in shape as its name suggests?  The Shread Mill is something of a puzzle.  Was it one of the two horse mills that were on the demesne in 1547 when Pedro de Gamboa took over the manor?  Possibly it was a saw mill.

There were thirteen head copyhold tenements in the hands of only four men: Richard Franklyn, Thomas Nicholl; Warner Norwood and his half-brother, Thomas Tailor.  Several of the head tenements had cottages, outbuildings and parcels of land dependant on them.  The owner of the tenement was responsible to the lord of the manor's steward for the whole tenement and received rent from the occupiers of the cottages.  When John Burnell took a barn and yard by the highway at Great Stanmore, a parcel of Fyddells, he had to pay 8d per annum to Richard Franklyn, the owner, at Fyddells, which stood near the corner of the Broadway and Dennis Lane.  Fyddells survived until the 1930s when it had been given a new name, Kingsdale.

58. *When the above photograph was taken about 1930, Fiddles had changed considerably in appearance and had been used as a veterinary surgery for many years. It was called Kingsdale in its final years.*

59. *Below, Buckingham Cottage (possibly the head tenement, Mackrells) being demolished in 1961 to make way for Buckingham Parade.*

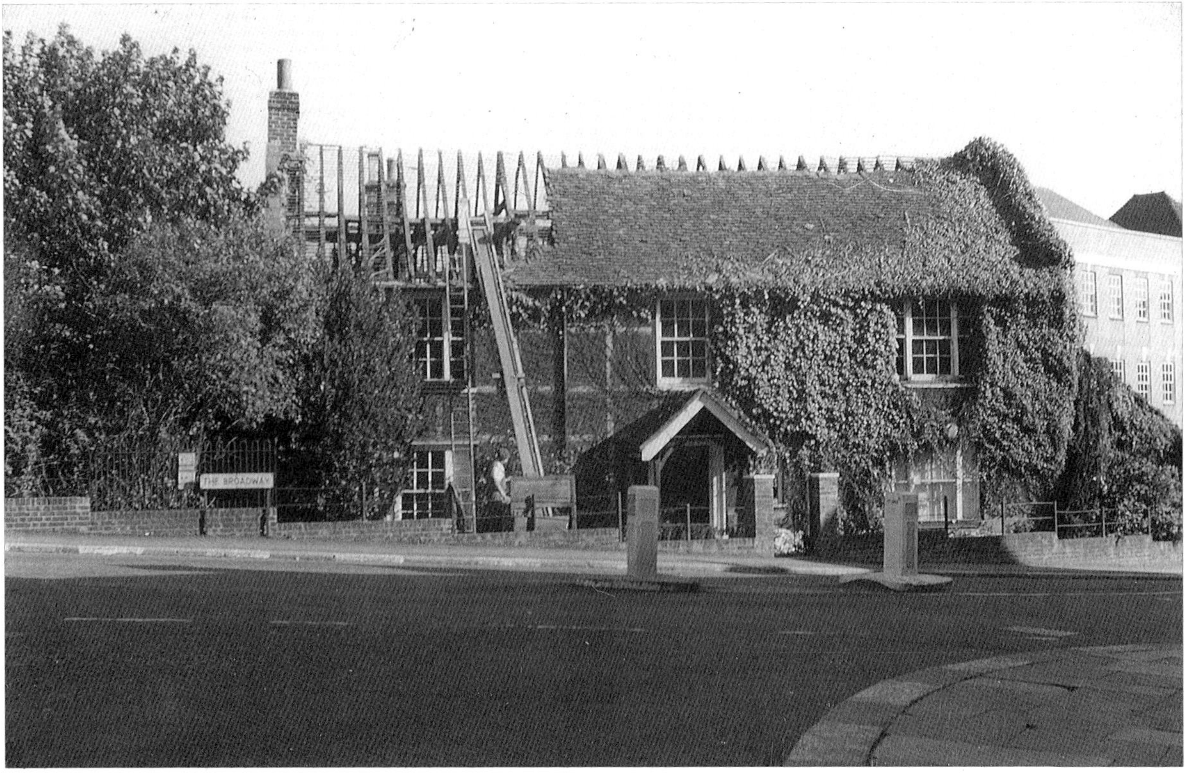

Warner Norwood paid quit rent on Aylwards, Mackrells alias Martyns, Mountegews, Goddards, Buggs and a cottage called Hodgkins. He had received them from his father, Thomas Norwood of Pinner between 1580 and 1583, along with two cottages, Lincolns and Pettits which were parcels of the head tenement, Pynnacles; and another cottage, Snowdons, parcel of the tenement called Thrums. Snowdons had gone to Henry Winch in 1584 and Mackrells was let on a 21-year lease to Robert Leycroft in the same year. The Norwoods' interest in Aylwards must have been on a small portion only. The quit rent was only 2d. The court roll for 1584 records the admission of Thomas Aylward to the tenement, Aylwards. His father, Michael Aylward had died twenty years earlier, leaving the property in the charge of his wife, Elinor, until his son, came of age. In 1586 Thomas sold it to Robert Leycroft. Aylwards stood west of Stanmore Hill, where Aylwards Close is now. Montagues was on the south side of the Broadway next to Pathgate (now Cottrell's Cottages) and was replaced by a new house about 1740. Buggs stood north-west of the church somewhere in the region of the Boot Pond and its site as well as Hodgkins was later swallowed up in Andrew Drummond's

*60. Aylwards stood on the west side of Stanmore Hill. This photograph, taken about 1930, shows the house shortly before it was demolished. The building had undergone many alterations since it was described as one of the head tenements of Great Stanmore in the 16th century. Aylmer Drive is on the site.*

Stanmore Park. Mackrells was sold to John Rogers, lord of the manor in 1713 and it passed to the Earl of Carnarvon in 1717. It may have stood on the junction of Stanmore Hill and Broadway and become the later Buckingham Cottage which was demolished in 1961.

Thomas Tailor, held Syme Rooks, Thrums and Pynnacles. A long building with a classical facade on the corner of Church Road and Green Lane was called Pynnacles. It was the home of the Tennent family in the nineteenth century and was burned down in 1930. However, plans and other references in the court rolls suggest that the early Pynnacles was quite near the corner of Church Road and Stanmore Hill and the name was applied to much of the land in the triangle formed by Green Lane, Church Road and Stanmore Hill.

Thomas Nicholl who was related to the Franklyns, had Braynes alias Pasgate, Rooks, Semons alias Barretts and Cockallens. Pasgate or Pathesgate stood on the corner of Marsh Lane and the Broadway and is the only one of the head tenements to remain in Stanmore to this day. It is now known as Cottrell's Cottages. The original name may have come from the Parkgate family mentioned in the fourteenth and fifteenth centuries. Cockallens and Barretts were simply fields in the seventeenth century situated on the west side of the green lane leading to Belmont.

The demesne was divided into five estates. The lord of the manor was living at the manor house with its garden, orchard and enclosed land; Taylors Close 5 acres, Great Highfield 12 acres, Long Downs and Flipshot 15 acres and Stocking 8 acres.

Englishes, with a barn, stable, orchard and garden was occupied by Robert Leycroft, with 10 acres of meadow called Kingdoms and Hook Mead, Crowshot 3 acres, Moorshot 4 acres, Frithfield 7 acres, Hawe Mead Close 6 acres and 11 acres in the common fields. Edmund Needham occupied the Brewhouse with two cottages attached and with a garden and a 1-acre meadow, two closes of pasture 9 acres, Russ Grove 4 acres, Great Shornes 11 acres and 3 closes, Long Downs, Little Downs and Underhill and 45 acres in the common fields of Harrow. Richard Fletcher, gentleman, had a tenement called Kingdoms with a barn, stable and little pightle of meadow 2 acres, Long Shornes 8 acres and land in Benehill Fields. Henry Edlyn had a messuage sometime called Pages with a garden and close on the backside 3 acres, a meadow and 3 acres in Borrowhill Field.

## THE BURNELLS

The family of John Burnell of the Clothworkers' Company, who leased the manor from 1599, acquired eight of the head tenements in the seventeenth century and became the most prominent family by mid-century, only to fade away from Stanmore altogether by 1700, leaving behind a monument in the church and a charity that still exists. The first John Burnell to have property in Stanmore was born about 1527, his father being another John Burnell of Dover. His wife, Barbara, was about 25 years younger and it was after their marriage in the 1570s that they came to Stanmore. They probably lived at Pathgate, the tenement which was eventually left to their eldest son.

John Burnell remained very much a citizen of London with interests in the City and its institutions, as his will, written in 1603 shows.[9] He had all his goods, chattels etc. appraised and divided into three equal portions according to the ancient custom of the City. One portion went to his wife, the second was divided equally among his five surviving children and the third was for the payment of his funeral expenses and legacies. Christ's Hospital, Bridewell, St Bartholomew's Hospital and St Thomas's received bequests and the poor prisoners in four City prisons. The Clothworkers' Company was left money for a dinner on the day of his burial and £100 to be used as loans for four-year terms to two young freemen who were not yet of the livery. The company was asked to devote the interest on the £100 to a bread charity at St Michael's, Crooked Lane and at Stanmore and any residue to provide coals for poor clothworkers.

The will supplies much information about his family. The sons were John, Thomas and William.

61.  *Pathgate from the front, a splendid jettied timber-framed building.  It belonged to the Burnell family in the 17th century, and was divided into two parts in the 18th century.  The Duke of Chandos owned the eastern end.  That portion was used as a farm house called Ward's Farm, Manor Farm and Old Church Farm at different times.*

62.  *Pathgate from the back, showing a staircase wing in the centre.  The westernmost bay was demolished in 1865.  The doors and windows are later insertions when the tenement was used as cottages.  The building was in danger of demolition in the 1960s, but was restored by Mr Cottrell in 1968 and converted into offices, now known as Cottrell's Cottages.*

*63. Pynnacles, the house where Lt Col. Hamilton Tovey-Tennent, and later the Wickens sisters lived. After it was burnt down in 1930 as seen here, the road was widened and now runs much closer to the site which is occupied by Cherchefelle Mews (built 1989). The early Pynnacles was near the corner of Church Road and Stanmore Hill.*

His daughters were married, Katherine to Thomas Morley by whom she had three daughters and Anne who had one daughter and was pregnant again at the time the will was written, to Richard Ball. Barbara Burnell's sister, Curdela, was married to John Swister, who occurs in the Stanmore records, and John Burnell's own sister was married to John Cage. Among his cousins was a Willoughby of Dover, but whether he or she was related to Baptist Willoughby the vicar of Stanmore is uncertain.

John Burnell died a wealthy man, leaving nearly £2500 in money, apart from mourning gowns and rings, and six tenements and 74 acres in addition to the lease of the manor. Two of the tenements were in Little Stanmore and held on lease and seventeen acres were called Shoelands and lay in Hendon. The tenements are not all named, but include Pathgate, Fiddells and Buggs which were left to the three sons. Barbara, his wife and executrix, inherited the lease of the manor.

John, the eldest son, died in January 1623, eight years before his mother. There is a very long religious preamble to his will possibly suggesting that he was a Puritan.[10] The Burnells were connected by marriage to the Bourchier family, one of whose members was Oliver Cromwell's wife and they had other Puritan friends. Thomas's wife, Hester nee Wollaston, left money to Dr Samuel Annesley and his wife, 'if it shall please God that I dye at [his] house'. Dr Annesley was a Puritan divine and rector of St Giles, Cripplegate during the Commonwealth. Like his father, John left money to the City hospitals and prisons and to the poor of a City parish (All Hallows, Barking, where he seems to have lived some of the time) and to needy persons in Stanmore. He speaks lovingly of his wife, Anne, 'earnestly requiringe her care for the educacon of my Children [six of them] in the feare of god and knowledge of vertue, both during her widowhood and after, when it may please god she joyne herself to another husband'. He left her the free use of the house in Stanmore (Pathgate) 'where I was born' during the minority of their eldest son and £300 and all her chains, bracelets and other jewels for herself. There is a hint that his youngest brother, William, was a little wild. He was left £20 'desiring him to remember my often admonitions unto him and before too late to make some good use thereof'. He appointed his other brother, Thomas, and brother-in-law, Thomas Morley, his executors along with his wife. His other brother-in-law, Richard Ball, was already dead and John had been administering his estate on behalf of his sister and her children.

64.  *A rural scene in Stanmore about 1920 showing haymaking in progress at Canons Park Farm.  Hay became a popular crop in the 19th century because of the enormous market for it in London.*

65.  *Pynnacles Place at the top of Green Lane.  The plaque gives the date 1822. The land of the head tenement called Pynnacles probably extended up the hill.*

*66. Goodalls stood next to the rectory on Colliers Lane (now Rectory Road). James Dalton, then rector, bought it in 1752 and it later became part of the Stanmore Park property. When Frederick Gordon's estates were put up for auction in 1909, the site of Goodalls was occupied by the Homestead, built about 1900. This was the home of Professor Guy Crowden and his wife, Jean, from the 1930s and renamed Wolstenholme. In the late 1960s it became a retirement home. The foundations of Goodalls were discovered in the late 1980s during the building operations for a new wing.*

Barbara Burnell, the first John's widow, established a charitable bequest to supply gowns to six poor women and bread for twelve poor people. The women were to come from Stanmore on alternate years. Two from Bushey, two from Harrow Weald and two from Edgware were to benefit in the other years. Her son, Thomas, added extra money for clothes and also for the supply of cheese in 1655.

The Stanmore registers say that William Burnell 'departed this life the 15th day of February being Saturday and was buried in the vault in the chancell the Thursday following being the 20th day of February 1644'. There is no comment on his character, such as accompanies the burial entry of his wife. 'Buried Elizabeth Burnell widdow and late wife of Mr William Burnell of this parish beinge a Gentlewoman of admirable parts and full of good works was buried in the vault within the church with the General Lamentations of those that know her: The 14th day January Anno Domini 1647'. [11]

The first John Burnell's great-grandson, John Bourchier, who owed attendance at the manor court at Great Stanmore in 1671 and his granddaughter, Ann Cook, were the only members of the family still to have property in the parish at that date. The male lines had died out.

## SOCIAL LIFE

Social life was regulated to a certain extent by the manor courts during the sixteenth and seventeenth centuries. Widow Weedon and Widow Harcott were publicly shamed by having their names recorded as common scolds in 1584, while Thomas Chapman was said to be a man of scandalous and ill behaviour who attends to no honest employment to support himself and his family. Widow Harcott had been before the courts a few years earlier in the lifetime of her husband, Richard, when she had been written down as 'a Common Breaker and Cutter of Hedges and a Destroyer of the Green wood of the Lord of the Mannor'.

The inhabitants of Great Stanmore were not permitted, on pain of a one shilling fine, to take in lodgers in case they became a charge on the parish. Nor were they allowed to supplement their income by gambling. 'Any person apprehended at any tables or other unlawful games for money within the precinct of this court shall forfeit to the lord for every offence 3s 4d'. John and Thomas Norwood were fined for taking hares with greyhounds in the 1630s. Bowls, however, seems to have been a popular and acceptable pastime, as an acre was enclosed from the common in 1637 by special request, to be 'made fit for the use of bowling and so kept'.

67. *The view from Warren House.*

# Woods and Warren

## WOODLANDS

By 1754, when John Rocque published his map of Middlesex, the heavily wooded hillsides of Great and Little Stanmore, which had provided sufficient forage for 1600 pigs in the late eleventh century, had been gradually cleared of trees. Not much more was left in Little Stanmore than a swathe of woodland probably comprising the present Pear Wood, Cloisters Wood and the area that is now the grounds of the Royal National Orthopaedic Hospital. Rocque called the wood on the north side of Wood Lane, Crabtree Orchard, and left the other unnamed. Only what appears to be the extended hedge called Long Hedge (unnamed on the map) is shown in Great Stanmore. Later the Long Hedge became Heriots Wood, straddling the parish boundary between Great Stanmore and Harrow Weald. The Tithe Award and Map of 1838 give about sixty acres of woodland in Little Stanmore and 83 acres in Great Stanmore.[1]

Plenty of field names suggest clearance. Nether and Over Ridding (an area ridded of trees), Frith Closes (frith is from an old English word meaning wood) and Thorn Croft, were all part of Great Stanmore's demesne lands in the sixteenth century. Several field names ended in 'grove', which means a little wood. Page's Grove, Stocking Grove Field, Bush Grove, Hasle (hazel?) Grove and Culver Grove were all mentioned in Great Stanmore in 1680.[2] Page's Grove lay between Cloisters Wood and Dennis Lane and had become Upper and Lower Dennis Field by 1815.[3] Little Stanmore had Bartholomew Grove, Cheyneisgrove, Wrennesgrove and Wolman Grove in 1540 and Bromfield Grove, Anmers Grove and Giles Park together covering 310 acres in 1589,[4] all cleared by the mid-18th century. Another woodland later lost was the strangely named Wapats or Wabbets Wood near the common. It was named in 1520 and was still part of the demesne of Great Stanmore in the seventeenth century.

Today's Pear Wood and Cloisters Wood are the same acreage as in 1838. Pear Wood may take its name from William Parys who owned 35 acres of woodland on Brockley Hill in 1277. In 1552 it was called Pear or Pares Wood which suggests the derivation. Cloisters was being let by St Bartholomew's Priory, along with the manor house of Canons in 1540.[5] Both woods were part of the demesne lands and were sold as part of the settled estate of Henry, Duke of Chandos in 1740. Subsequent owners were Thomas Sharpe (the Duke of Chandos's secretary), Joshua Sharpe and James Forbes who owned the Warren House and the forerunner of Stanmore Hall.[6]

For a time the woods were part of the Stanmore

*68. This watercolour was painted in May 1870 from the grounds of Warren House and shows the wooded landscape.*

Hall estate, but were attached to Warren House again by 1851.[7] In 1998 the woods are privately owned, but there is public access from Dennis Lane, Wood Lane, Kerry Avenue and the Golf Range in Brockley Hill. The woods show some of the features, such as plentiful bluebells, associated with ancient woodland. There has clearly been much digging in them over the years, probably for gravel which lies on the surface in some places.

Many of the medieval woodlands of north-west Middlesex such as those at Ruislip and Harefield, were composed of oak timber trees with a hornbeam underwood which was coppiced in rotation to produce long poles suitable for pea and bean sticks, wattles and kindlewood. The oaks were usually grown to provide timber for houses and furniture. There is no evidence of coppiced hornbeam in the Stanmore woods today, but there is some hazel which was also coppiced and treated as underwood. St Bartholomew's Priory had 56½ acres of woodland in which the underwood was worth 13s 1d in 1306. Maybe it was hazel. There were always problems balancing the two types of productivity. If large oaks predominated in a patch of woodland the underwood was unable to grow through lack of light and space. When oak was cut the underwood

tended to take over and prevent new growth. A further difficulty was that much of the medieval woodland where animals could graze was unenclosed; this is now known as wood pasture. Tender oak saplings and the new coppice growth were eaten by grazing domesticated animals like sheep and by the wild deer. The large area of common land on the top of Stanmore Hill was probably denuded of trees because of the grazing and the felling of oak for sale. Other areas like the Riddings were probably deliberately ridded of their trees to create pasture. The surviving woodlands were enclosed with banks and ditches and taken into the large estates.

The groves were small, usually not more than two acres and may have been planted with specific trees like hazel. Another type of wood mentioned in Stanmore's records is the hedge that is allowed to develop into a strip of woodland. Long Hedge survives on Stanmore Hill in Heriots Wood and there was a Broad Hedge in Little Stanmore in 1277 belonging to William Parys.

A glance at the map of Middlesex in 1754 by Rocque, who was interested in garden design, shows another source of timber in the long avenues planted in geometric patterns all over the Canons estate and up Brockley Hill and in Stanmore Park

*69. A view from Brockley Hill over Pear Wood and Cloisters Wood.*

## USING THE TIMBER

Timber was used for building houses and for repairing houses and barns. The Duke of Chandos made provision in his leases for the tenants to have timber for repairs (housebote). It is probable that timber from Stanmore was sold in medieval times to help repair buildings at Smithfield, but no records survive.

Colliers Lane, the road leading west from Church Road, suggests that there may have been some charcoal burning going on in Stanmore. Equally the colliers may have been working on Harrow Weald and using the lane through Stanmore to transport their products.

A book[8] giving particulars of the timber, wood and bark sold off by the Chandos estate in Middlesex in the years 1782-5 sheds more light on the values and sizes of the trees being felled in the late eighteenth century. The Middlesex estate included land in Edgware and at Winchmore Hill and Stanmore. The wood and timber came from gardens and fields as well as woods. The timber was sorted into three sizes: over 35 feet, 20-35 feet and 20 feet and under. Most of it (about 75%) was 20 feet and under in length. Only a tiny proportion of the trees were over 35 feet.

The wood or underwood was sold as bush faggots, bakers' bavins, shides, faggots, talwood and timber tops. Faggots were supposed to be 3 feet long and were composed of bundles of sticks that were too small to burn by themselves. The bavins were types of faggots made from small underwood or the brushwood and spray of large underwood, or from the lop and top of timber trees. Some were specially made for bread ovens and therefore called bakers' bavins. All the faggots were enclosed with hazel twig or withy (willow), tied into a complicated knot. Talwood, from the Norman French *'boys de taille'* meaning coppice wood, was a log about 4 feet long and 20 inches in girth, while the shides were also logs from the branches of timber trees.

Bark peeled from oak was sold to tanneries in each year covered by the book, realising varying amounts from £69 to £123.

Elm trees growing in Green Lane, Stanmore, were felled in 1783 and some fir from a garden and ash and chestnut, presumably from hedgerows are also mentioned. The best year from a financial point of view was 1784, when the sale of wood, timber and bark realised £903 10s 6d.

Sales of wood were advertised in newspapers. In 1808 Mr Fitch, a wine-merchant of Jermyn Street, advertised a sale of nearly 3000 timber trees in Pear Wood 'between Brockley Hill and Stanmore' to be held at the Abercorn Arms on 15th and 16th March. They included oak, ash, beech, fir, lime, arbele (white poplar) and other trees. 2000 had their lop, top and bark, but not the beech which had already been felled. The rest were numerically marked with paint and would be sold by the foot, measured when felled. Richard Fitch, a Stanmore auctioneer, would conduct the sale and applications to view the trees were to be made at Woodgate House by Crabtree Orchard.

## THE COMMON

Stanmore Common, formerly called Bushey Heath, today stretches along the county boundary and south to the Watford Road, covering 120 acres, the same area as shown on the Tithe Award map of 1838. There was also Stanmore Marsh nowadays reduced to a ten-acre strip, but formerly much more extensive.

The common and heathland was a useful source of fuel and building materials for the people of Stanmore, but their rights to cut turf and furze and dig gravel were sometimes disputed by the lord of the manor. Gravel digging was permitted on the common, but only for the repair of tenements. Thomas Burnell and John Norwood were both presented at the manor court for taking gravel, presumably for other purposes, in 1637. It is likely that these more influential tenants of the manor sold gravel to their own profit and the lord of the manor's loss. They were fined twenty shillings each, but the fines were respited because the jury said that the digging of gravel was a customary right. The purpose for which gravel might be dug continued to be in dispute and a court of survey in 1679 and 1680 finally set out all the customs of the manor. Copy-

*70. The settlement at Little Common probably began with encroachments upon the common. This view across Spring Pond shows ornamental cottages surrounding the stableyard of Stanmore Hall. They were probably built by Robert Hollond about 1860, but are on the site of earlier cottages and gardens which belonged to the Fitch family.*

hold tenants were said to have been 'used tyme out of mind to have and take Furses, Heath, gravell and such like things growing and being upon the said Comons or Wasts for their fuel and necessary uses', a suitably vague purpose.[9] The gravel was the most valuable commodity, especially in the eighteenth century when the Kilburn turnpike trust was a good customer.

The Duke of Chandos's steward, John Brocket, took three legal opinions on the long-held customary right and tried to curtail it in 1725. The Duke obviously exploited the common himself. In August 1738 he leased his lime kilns, brick kilns, lime pits, clay pits and chalk pits to Thomas Pond of Bushey along with five acres of land for 21 years, agreeing at the same time to allow Thomas to build a house there for his convenience.[10]

From the court rolls we learn that cottages were being erected upon the waste in the 1580s. The one to which Richard Hughes was admitted in 1584 was at Green Lane and had half a rod of land enclosed by a hedge.[11] These encroachments were often permitted to remain and were only occasionally ordered to be pulled down. A number of cottages built in the seventeenth century probably formed the nucleus of the hamlet of Little Common. It was

*71. Maytree Cottage at Little Common. This 18th-century cottage was probably one of the alehouses recorded there in Victorian times. Alfred Franklyn sold beer at the William the Fourth in 1851 as well as being a carpenter.*

*72. Little Common. This house stands behind The Vine.*

cut off from the rest of the common by the bowling green (about where the cricket club is now) and today forms a pleasant rural enclave with many decorative cottages of various dates from the seventeenth century (no. 3) to 1970 (nos. 44 & 45) scattered around the impressive former stables of Stanmore Hall.

Tenants were allowed to graze their own animals on the common and marsh, but hogs had to be

*73. Old Joe Hill, the keeper of the Common in the 1920s.*

ringed (to prevent them digging up the ground) all the year and had to be kept yoked from Christmas until the end of harvest. Stanmore marsh was considered to belong to Great Stanmore, though it straddled the boundary and was a constant temptation to the people of Little Stanmore. The tenants of five Little Stanmore tenements, presumably all on Edgware High Street since three of them were inns, the Falcon, the Crown, the Lion, Hall's and Nicholl's, had the right of common pasture on the marsh for six sheep each, but no other kind of beast in 1582. Reiteration of these rules suggests that they were frequently broken.

## THE WARREN

The coney (rabbit) warren on Stanmore Common was 44 acres 2 roods and 28 perches in extent in 1714. The warren house and yard, a 14-acre arable field called Page's ground and four closes called Thrifts, went with it. William Adams was then the warrener. Although warreners in medieval times looked after and protected the rabbits which belonged to the lord, eighteenth-century warreners in Stanmore had much more extensive duties relating to the woodlands and general manorial administration. The Duke of Chandos's warrener's business in 1740 was set out as follows:[12]

STANMORE COMMON.

74. *Animals often strayed from their pastures and were impounded lest they damage growing crops. This 18th-century print shows the pound at Stanmore.*

'He is to have under his care the preservation of the woods, to walk round them frequently in the week to see that the fences and hedges are duly kept up and preserved and to use his utmost endeavours to discover who shall break them down or steal them, that the persons so offending may be convicted and punish'd as the law requires; and particularly to take care that no wood cut down for faggotting and stacking be stolen or carried off and for his care and due discharge of his duty he is to have one shilling in the pound for all the wood that shall be sold or brought to Cannons for the use of the family.

He is to be bailiff of the manors of Stanmore Magna and Stanmore Parva and to collect in all the chief rents of the said manors and in regard the amount thereof is but small and the distance between the parties who pay'em remote from each other, he is to receive half a crown in the pound for his pains. He is also to receive the money for the gravel, turf and mold that shall be sold upon the Heath and Waste, and for his pains and trouble herein, he is to have the same allowance of half a crown in the pound provided he suffers none to be carried off except by such to whom the Duke gives leave to have it gratis, or who shall pay for it before it is taken away, except for the gravel for the statute work which is paid for by the parishes once a year.

He is likewise to have the Warrenhouse to live in and the Warren and benefit of the Rabbits for the first two years gratis, after which he is to pay the rent of [*sic*] per annum for the same, but he is to take particular care that the Duke has the refusal of the young rabbits at 18d a couple: and in regard the Warren is at present in a very bad condition, the Duke is willing for his further encouragement and to enable him the better to stock it and bring it into good order to allow him for the first two years the sum of £4 a year.

Furthermore he is to have the charge of the Pound and to take care that Justice be done to the Duke and to every other person who may be affected thereby having their cattle pounded.'

The later history of the Warren House is discussed on pp70-72.

75. *(top left)  Stanmore Common in the 1920s.*

76. *(below)  The Warren House. This small cottage, possibly timber-framed beneath the facade, with a brick chimney and what could be a bread oven beside it, appears to have been the warrener's house.*

77. *(above)  The later grand Warren House was largely the creation of Sir Robert Smirke and is now the Islamic Centre.*

78. *James Forbes's house at Stanmore Hill. He placed oriental sculptures in a pagoda in his gardens which extended to Dennis Lane.*

# 'Beset with Gentlemen's Houses'

Writing on the 23rd December 1888, William Morris described the country around Stanmore as 'pretty after a fashion, very well wooded and up and down: but much beset with gentlemen's houses'. His company had a commission to prepare tapestries for one of those houses, Stanmore Hall, and he was on his way to visit it. The ambience of the place was not

in tune with his socialist soul. He continued 'Our client sent his carriage to meet me and I couldn't help laughing to see the men I met touching their hats, clearly not to me, but to it.'[1] The gentrification of Stanmore which so disturbed Morris started during the eighteenth century as houses or cottages on the Canons estate were granted to rich London and East India merchants and bankers who transformed former meadow, woodland and common into plantations and pleasure grounds and enlarged and modernised the buildings. Smaller decorative houses appeared on the lower part of Stanmore Hill, which probably became used as a main road only after the Duke of Chandos created the new London Road along the north side of Canons Park in 1718. Several of the head tenements in Great Stanmore

79. *James Forbes (1749-1819) of the East India Company, who lived at Dower House (forerunner of Stanmore Hall) on Stanmore Hill.*

which had belonged to the Burnells and their relatives in Stuart times were also refurbished during the next hundred years or so and became suitable for the retired gentry and superior tradesmen who appeared on the Stanmore scene. Several of the houses were adapted to become academies to provide an education for the gentlemen's sons.

## WARREN HOUSE, DOWER HOUSE AND THE BOWLING GREEN HOUSE

Three houses built or owned by James Brydges, 1st Duke of Chandos, are of particular interest: the Warren House, the Dower House and the Bowling Green House. James Forbes bought the first two about 1780[2], and the Dower House developed into Stanmore Hall. This should not be confused with another house near it lower down Stanmore Hill which was given the name Dower House in 1923.

James Forbes (1749-1819) was in the service of the East India Company from 1765 to 1784 and while living in India took a great interest in all aspects of the life of the country. He returned to England in the 1780s with an enormous number of notebooks filled with landscapes and drawings of animals, plants and religious objects, which he used to create a book, *Oriental Memoirs,* which was published between 1813-15. A colleague in the East India Company, John Dalton, had married his sister and

all three came to Stanmore where Dalton's brother, James, was rector from 1781. It was probably in preparation for his retirement from the Company that Forbes had already in 1780 purchased part of the settled estates of Henry, 2nd Duke of Chandos[3]: the Warren House, Cloisters Wood and a house and grounds on the corner of Stanmore Hill and Wood Lane, which had been built by the 1st Duke of Chandos for use by his wife during her widowhood should she survive him – in effect a Dower House.

## THE DOWER HOUSE

James Forbes married Rose Gaylord, daughter of Joseph Gaylord of Stanmore and by 1788 the two couples were settled in the Dower House, though he had a town house in Albemarle Street. The Brahmins of Hindustan had presented him with groups of oriental sculpture as 'a greatful acknowledgement of his benevolent attention to their happiness during a long residence among them',[4] and this he placed in an octagonal temple or pagoda specially erected in his garden which extended to Dennis Lane. The sculptures probably excited a good deal of comment because Lysons remarked that they "are very ancient and the only specimens of Hindoo sculpture in this island.'[5]

About 1800 Forbes bought the tongue of land between Dennis Lane and Cloisters Wood, joining the latter with the Warren House and his other land on the slopes of Stanmore Hill.[6] Shortly afterwards, taking advantage of the break in the Napoleonic wars brought about by the Peace of Luneville and Treaty of Amiens (1802), he went to France, but was caught there when war broke out again and was imprisoned for two years. His daughter was married to a French émigré, the Comte de Montalembert, and their son, who was brought up by his grandfather, became a well-known medieval historian. After the wars finally ended in 1815 Forbes probably spent much time in France and indeed died at Aix-la-Chapelle in 1819. He sold the Dower House, the Dennis Fields and Cloisters Wood to Roger Elliot Roberts of Upper Grosvenor Street, a colonel in the service of the East India Company in 1815.[7]

General Alexander Campbell of Monzie, Perthshire purchased the copyhold part of the estate in 1820 and presumably the freehold house as well and Edward Orme of Bayswater bought the estate in 1825[8] but sold it to the trustees of the marriage settlement of Lieutenant General Sir John Lambert who fought at Waterloo, in 1828. Lambert's name appears as owner on the Sayer map of 1827, which strangely shows no house on the site. From him it went to Thomas Teed of Argill House, Richmond, Surrey in 1835[9] who sold the Dower House in 1842 to Matthew John Rhodes.

*80. An aerial view of Stanmore Hall in March 1935. A conservatory and farm buildings can be seen on the right. A new house has been erected on the Stanmore Hall frontage on the left. Directly above the turret of the hall beyond the trees rises Hill House.*

The plan accompanying the memorial of the transaction in the Middlesex Land Registry shows the house the same shape and size and the pleasure grounds with a lake and Mr Forbes's octagonal temple, the same as on the plan of 1815 when it had been sold to Colonel Roberts. But in the intervening years the stable yard had been laid out as a garden, presumably the kitchen garden. The main driveway to the front door of the house came in from Stanmore Hill, with an entrance to the stables and offices from Wood Lane. Only the land within the compass of Stanmore Hill, Wood Lane and Dennis Lane was acquired by Mr Rhodes.

## STANMORE HALL

The next year Rhodes set about building a splendid gothic pile, replete with battlements and turrets more or less across the site of the kitchen garden. This new building was Stanmore Hall and replaced the Dower House which was demolished about 1850. The architect was the Irishman, John Macduff Derick (1810-61) who was better known for his ecclesiastical work. A matching lodge, which still stands in Wood Lane, was occupied by Susan Day, the cook and her husband at the time of the 1851 census. Thomas Teed's daughter, Ellen Julia, had married Robert Hollond MP for Hastings in 1840. He is famous on account of his interest in aeronautical science and a journey which he made in a hot air balloon from Vauxhall Gardens to Nassau in the Netherlands in 1836. The Hollonds purchased the new hall in 1847 and made it their chief home, but they were often abroad. Mrs Hollond was of a liberal turn of mind and interested in social and welfare work. She had a salon in Paris where she entertained other liberals and she founded the first crèche in London in 1844. Her husband died in 1877 and was buried in an ornate mausoleum in the old church. The decorative cottage beside the churchyard of Great Stanmore on the Uxbridge Road, designed by Brightwen Binyon, was built as a memorial to him in 1881, the land having been conveyed to Mrs Hollond by Lord Wolverton of Stanmore Park. Robert Hollond is also commemorated in a window on the south side of the present

*81. A cherub adorning the doorway to the garden at Stanmore Hall.*

church.  Mrs Hollond died at the hall in 1884.

During the Hollonds' occupation new farm build-ings were erected on Wood Lane directly opposite the Spring Pond and a new laundry, stables and ornamental cottages were built on Little Common about 1863, the latter on the site of older cottages and gardens.[10] Two older cottages near the laundry called Woodbine Cottage and Springlands and The Cottage (confusingly called the Dower House later) adjoining the hall on the south in Stanmore Hill, were also part of the estate, but were leased out rather than being occupied by servants and work-ers. Springlands had its own stable and coach house. The Cottage also had a stable and a gardener's cottage and nearly five acres of meadow, while Woodbine Cottage had outbuildings.  There were two other cottages with a plantation and meadow and the detached farm lodge in Dennis Lane was on the site of the present Hall Farm Drive.

Mr Hollond had also bought up property at the bottom of Stanmore Hill, including The Queen's Head, a baker's and a fishmonger's shops and two gentlemen's houses, Syon House and Elm House, the latter, now 17 Stanmore Hill, with a coach house beside the entrance gates.

*82. A series of photographs of Stanmore Hall were taken in 1891 to record the alterations and redecoration undertaken by Mr Knox D'Arcy. This picture shows the gothic library rather sparsely furnished with books.*

83. *The laundry built by Robert Hollond c1863 on Little Common.*

Mrs Hollond's nephew John Robert Hollond put the Hall and considerable estate up for auction in 1888. The Hall, farm and service buildings were purchased by William Knox D'Arcy, a solicitor, who had shares in a 'mountain of gold,' the Mount Morgan Gold Mining Company in Queensland and who had also struck oil in the Anglo-Persian oilfield in 1889. He employed Brightwen Binyon, to extend the house and William Morris to work on the interior. Morris was rather patronising about Stanmore Hall and the architect, writing of them on 10 June 1890 as 'a sham Gothic house of 50 years ago now being added to by a young architect of the commercial type – men who are very bad. Fancy in one room there was not a pane of glass that opened.'[11] Brightwen Binyon, originally from Manchester, was a pupil of Alfred Waterhouse and had a practice in Ipswich. He chiefly designed libraries, schools and town halls which may account for Morris's jibe. Binyon's first work in Stanmore had been at the Grove in the 1870s for Mr and Mrs Brightwen. The tapestries produced by Morris & Co., on the theme of the search for the Holy Grail, were designed by Edward Burne-Jones and were hung in the dining room. After Mr D'Arcy's death in 1917 they were sold, but a later version of five of the six panels are now in the Birmingham Art Gallery.

84. *The ornamental cottages and stables built by Robert Hollond c1863 on the site of older cottages on Little Common.*

Mr D'Arcy and his second wife lived at the Hall, but also had a town house in Grosvenor Square. A society item in the *Times* announcing that they had arrived there 'from the country' went on to describe Mrs D'Arcy as 'a tall, slim, handsome woman, with an abundance of pale golden hair. She is a good bridge player and a quite exceptionally graceful dancer'.

After D'Arcy's death the house passed into public use. It is said to have been used as an assize court,

*85. Hollond Cottage by the churchyard, erected by Julia Hollond in 1881 in memory of her husband, Robert.*

then as flats in the 1930s. During the Second World War it was the Officers' Mess for the staff of the Allied Expeditionary Air Force HQ at Bentley Priory, and known irreverently by them as Gremlin Castle. It was used as a nurses' home for the Royal National Orthopaedic Hospital from 1947 to 1971 after which its fate hung in the balance and many people feared that it would be demolished and the site redeveloped, especially after a fire in 1979. However, local pressure and a changing attitude towards conservation prevailed and the house was sympathetically restored and converted into offices. Unfortunately an unhappily sited recent addition is very obtrusive and spoils the view of the picturesque roofline from Little Common.

## A PEW IN GREAT STANMORE CHURCH

Dating from the ownership of the Dukes of Chandos, possession of the Dower House and later Stanmore Hall, always included a pew at the south side of the gallery at the west end of the parish church of Great Stanmore and seats behind, for the Chandos family servants. The repair of this pew was the responsibility of the owners of Stanmore Hall.

*86. Elm House, 17 Stanmore Hill was added to the Stanmore Hall estate by Robert Hollond.*

## AYLWARDS

Aylwards (*see ill. 60*) lay back from the road just below the crest of Stanmore Hill. It was one of the old head tenements of the manor of Great Stanmore and was a yeoman's rather than a gentleman's house in the sixteenth and seventeenth centuries. It had belonged to the Norwoods and passed to a cousin, William Boys in 1711. The Revd John Boys of Redbourn, Hertfordshire, owned it in the middle of the eighteenth century and was succeeded by his son, Philip in 1788.[12] His son, Edward was still under-age when he took possession in 1803.

He appears to have divided the property into two. In 1823 he surrendered Aylwards at the Manor Court to John Marks of Great Portland Street who was a carriage dealer. About thirteen acres of land went with it, Holdens Orchard, the Lower Three Acres and Hill Field. Four years later Mr Boys sold a house 'lately divided into two messuages on Stanmore Hill' to Michael Foveaux of Sloane Street Esq. Garrets Field, Ash Orchard (then thrown together) and the Home Meadow (formerly the Upper Three Acres and Brown Field) were included. The fields sold to John Marks and Michael Foveaux together surround Aylwards. The house itself was probably remodelled at the time of the division. The widows of the two gentlemen sold out to the Marquess of Abercorn, Sarah Marks in 1843 and Mrs Foveaux in 1841.[13] The two halves were reunited by 1844 when Aylwards was leased by the Marquess to James Rhodes of Duncan Terrace, Islington, for 21

years. The whole tenement was sold to John Kelk, esq. in 1863, when Abercorn, who had already sold him most of the Bentley Priory estate, sold him also the lordship of the manor. When Mr Kelk left Stanmore, Aylwards was purchased by Mr Hollond of Stanmore Hall. It was sold in 1888 to Peter Clutterbuck esq. of the Brewery House.[14] The upper floor of the gardener's cottage had by then been converted into a billiard room.

The general manager of the London & North Western Railway, Sir Frederick Harrison, lived at Aylwards in the 1890s and afterwards Sir John D. Rees, a retired diplomat who had an admirable command of oriental languages. He gained his knighthood after crossing the House from the Liberal ranks to the Conservatives. He died in 1922 and was succeeded by his son, Sir Richard. Aylwards was demolished sometime after 1934, although the lodge was still standing in 1974. Aylmer Drive now occupies the former driveway and Aylwards Close is on the site of the house and gardens.

## THE WARREN HOUSE

A watercolour sketch[15] of the Warren House, executed in 1810, shows what was probably a timber-framed cottage of two bays, with a porch added at the front and an outshot at the back, although the timber frame is completely hidden under some form of rendering. A stepped brick chimney on one gable is probably original and a small chimney at the other

*87. The Warren House as extended by Robert Smirke.*

88. *Edward VII visiting the Bischoffsheims at Warren House in June 1907. Mr Bischoffsheim was already ill and died in March 1908.*

end appears to be an addition. What looks like the outside of a bread oven can be seen beside the chimney. The accommodation was possibly two rooms on each floor, with all the rooms capable of having fireplaces. The building as painted could well date from the seventeenth century.

The warrener is not heard of after the mid-18th century and his cottage was replaced with a small late-Georgian building, which stood in a commanding position with views sweeping over Stanmore towards London. During James Forbes's ownership he enclosed some waste on Wood Lane and let the the whole to Baker John Sellon of Stanmore, a Sergeant-at-Law in 1807 for 58 years,[16] which sounds like the remainder of a lease. Mr Forbes's trustees sold the Warren House to Sir Thomas Plumer, Master of the Rolls and the then owner of Canons, in 1822,[17] but Sir Robert Smirke, who was later to be architect of the British Museum and King's College, London, is shown as the owner on the 1827 Sayer map and the manor court rolls give him as the copyhold tenant of land around in 1826.[18] It was a most desirable spot for a country retreat and during his long ownership he altered the house considerably, his additions not being at all in his usual classical style, but Jacobean with Dutch gables in yellow brick. A *porte-cochère* is the most striking but not altogether pleasing feature of the house from Wood Lane.

Sir Robert leased Warren House to the Keyser family in 1851 and sold it to them in 1862. Charles E. Keyser, son of the purchaser, was chairman of the Colne Valley Water Company. When he left Stanmore for Aldermaston Manor near Reading in 1890, the Warren went to Henry Louis Bischoffsheim and his wife, daughter of Bierdeman, court jeweller at Vienna. The banking house of Bischoffsheim and Goldschmidt was well known in the City and the couple were leading members of the Prince of Wales's set. They lived at Bute House when in town. The Prince often visited them at Stanmore and later when he was king. Mr Bischoffsheim died in March 1906, leaving £100,000 to charities, but his widow lived on until 1922. She had been especially interested in horticulture, being well known for her carnations and her ability to raise orchid seedlings, but she had also enjoyed agriculture and had a famed herd of Jersey cows.[19]

She had two daughters and her grandson, Sir John FitzGerald, succeeded her. He was a member of the Middlesex Agricultural Council and also a Knight of Kerry. Combining these two interests he replaced the Jerseys with a herd of Kerries, kept in the most modern cowsheds and milk was produced under hygienic conditions. Either the Kerry cows or Sir John himself are remembered in Kerry Avenue on the 1930s Warren House estate. He was still living

*89. Bowling Green House near the present Stanmore Cricket Club. It had been built by the 1st Duke of Chandos by the bowling green and used as a banqueting house to entertain his friends.*

at Warren House in 1937 when most of the grounds (about 110 acres) including Cloisters Wood were purchased by Harrow Council to be part of the Green Belt and public open space.[20] Sir John remained as tenant after the house was bought by the Middlesex County Council and Harrow UDC in 1940. The National Corporation for the Care of Old People bought Warren House in 1951 and it became an old people's home called Springbok House, presumably because the purchase money came from the South Africa Gift to Britain Fund. It became a geriatric sub-unit of Edgware General Hospital in 1971 but was closed down in 1978. The Yakar Educational Trust purchased it with the intention of turning it into a Jewish Adult Education Centre, but nothing came of the scheme and the building stood empty and decaying for many years. Eventually the Khoja Shia Ithna-Asken Community took it over and it was fully restored and converted into an Islamic Training Centre which opened in 1987. It provides a day centre for the elderly, a nursery school for children, daily Koran classes for women and children, Arabic classes and weekly worship.

## BOWLING GREEN HOUSE

The 1st Duke of Chandos owned and probably re-built the Bowling Green House, more or less on the site of the present Stanmore Cricket Club ground. It was let to Samuel Symons along with the bowling green, for £10 a year in 1714[21] and was probably the same building where the young James Brydges had enjoyed convivial meals with friends after games of bowls in the 1690s, when he had been visiting his wife's aunt, Lady Drax, in Stanmore. Tradition has it that when Duke he used it as a Banqueting House to entertain his guests at Canons, but it was still officially called the Bowling Green House in 1753, although it was not then rented out, but retained in hand.[22] Later it was owned by George Heming, a member of a family which owned land in Hillingdon and Ruislip. Lysons in his volume on the parishes of Middlesex published in 1811, says that Mr Heming's widow was then in occupation and adds that the house stood on the highest spot of ground in the neighbourhood. According to the *Ambulator* magazine the house was demolished soon after 1820 and the house, like Stanmore Hall, is not

**STANMORE, MIDDLESEX.**

The Particulars and Conditions of Sale

OF VALUABLE

# FREEHOLD ESTATES,
## AT STANMORE,

INCLUDING

## THE BANQUETING HOUSE,

WITH OFFICES,

**Pleasure Grounds, Garden, and Paddocks of Meadow Land,**

CONTAINING

### NEARLY SIXTEEN ACRES.

## A RESIDENCE,

WITH

PLEASURE GROUND, GARDEN, & PADDOCK of MEADOW LAND,

THE WHOLE ABOUT TWO ACRES.

Late in the occupation of Mr. Cox.

## A Spacious Brick-built RESIDENCE,

*NOW DIVIDED INTO SEVERAL DWELLINGS,*

WITH

OUT-BUILDINGS, YARD, AND SMALL GARDENS,

Let to Mr. Kirby, and in the occupation of his Under-tenants.

### WHICH WILL BE SOLD BY AUCTION,

BY MESSRS.

## FAREBROTHER, CLARK and LYE,

At Garraway's Coffee House, 'Change Alley, Cornhill,

**On WEDNESDAY, the 16th day of JUNE, 1847,**

AT TWELVE O'CLOCK, IN THREE LOTS.

*90. Sale Particulars of the Banqueting/Bowling Green House in 1847.*

*91. The Cottage built in 1817 for Dr Hooper, on the site of the Rev. Edward Dwyer's boarding school. It was known as the Dower House from 1923 until its demolition c1955.*

shown on Sayer's map of 1827.

However, Bowling Green House and lands formed part of the settled estates of Richard Plantagenet, Duke of Buckingham and Chandos in 1839 and a Sale Brochure of the Duke's land in 1847 describes the Banqueting House and its sixteen acres and shows it on a plan.[23] It boasted a water closet on the first floor along with five sleeping rooms, a cheerful and spacious drawing room finished with French paper, a dining and breakfast room finished with crimson flock paper and an entrance hall. There were wine and coal cellars and a kitchen in the basement. It was already leased to Peter Clutterbuck with ten years yet to run, and Thomas Clutterbuck bought it for £1000. The manor court roll for 1852 refers to 'the Grove alias the Banqueting House', which is puzzling as the Grove and the Banqueting/Bowling Green House both existed in the eighteenth century and can hardly have been the same place. Thomas Clutterbuck seems to have demolished the Bowling Green House as it is not shown on the 1864 25-inch map. Richard Heming of Hillingdon, cousin of George Heming, still owned land with a pair of cottages on it, on the common in 1848.[24]

## THE COTTAGE

A man called Paul Vaillant owned 'a commodious dwelling house and boarding school' on the east side of Stanmore Hill at the turn of the nineteenth century, along with a house and shop nearby and a brick house opposite.[25] The dwelling house and boarding school was The Cottage lying immediately south of what became Stanmore Hall. The brick house opposite was probably the listed building that is now no. 23 Stanmore Hill. Mr Vaillant had several pieces of meadowland near the common as well and also by Marsh Lane and the Marsh. The whole was put up for sale in December 1803 and The Cottage was bought by the Revd Edward Dwyer who had just entered upon a nine-year lease of the same the previous Michaelmas. The Cottage had four bed-chambers and four upper apartments (probably attics), dining and breakfast parlour, school room, kitchen and other offices. Apparently the Academy was a separate building in the playground, which had its own gateway and entrance. We know nothing about the number of pupils who were accommodated.

Dr Hooper purchased it from Mr Dwyer in 1816 and rebuilt the house. A drawing of The Cottage at Stanmore was exhibited at the Royal Academy Exhibition in 1817, with the caption 'now building for Dr Hooper' under the direction of James Sanderson. Upon the death of Dr Hooper's son in 1852 it was bought by Mr Hollond and became part of the Stanmore Hall estate.[26]

# The Grove and The Limes

## THE GROVE

The Grove estate was created in the mid-eighteenth century on fields lying north-east of Stanmore Common called Upper, Lower, Little and Further Thrifts, granted to Jacob Pereira from the Duke of Chandos's demesne land in 1741.[1] He converted them into a plantation and pleasure ground called 'Mon Plaisir' and perhaps built the brick dwelling house. Mr Pereira's will, proved in 1760, shows him to have been a London merchant with connections with Amsterdam. He wished to be buried in the burial ground of the Portuguese Jews' Synagogue in London, and left money to the elders of that synagogue and another in Amsterdam. Moses, a younger son, was the residuary legatee named in the will dated 22 June 1759, but he was cut off with a shilling in a codicil written the following January 'having proved even worse than his elder brother'. Two daughters, Catherine and Rachel were to benefit instead provided they married according to the will of his executor or his second wife, Esther, of whom he speaks lovingly.

The Grove was advertised for sale in 1762 and bought by Aaron Capadose who had been a legatee of Mr Pereira's will. Discovering that the plantation called Mon Plaisir had been robbed of evergreens, he offered £5 reward for the apprehension of disorderly trespassers who destroyed the game, and warned in a newspaper that gins and gun-traps had been posted about the grounds. Mr Capadose died in 1782 leaving his niece, Hana de Jacob Capadose as his sole executrix and legatee. The parish register rather oddly, since he was Jewish and was buried in Amsterdam, mentions Aaron's death, saying that he was supposed to be 105 years of age. He was probably 95.

Brewer in his *Beauties of England & Wales* says that Capadose's successor in Stanmore was a German gentleman called Fierville who was an admirer of Rousseau. He is said to have constructed a lake between the house and common with an island in the middle with a tomb on it, similar to that of Rousseau on the Ile de Peupliers at Ermenonville. The water was drained later and trees and shrubs planted, leaving the raised tomb. The earth dug to create the lake had been piled into a mound and Herr Fierville built a very fashionable grotto on it with Hertfordshire pud-

92. *Eliza Brightwen (1830-1906), a popular naturalist who lived at The Grove from about 1872 until her death.*

ding stone. What was left was known in the 1930s as the Hunge. It was lined with red cockleshells and had an aviary and a fountain inside. Yet another earthwork from this period, both fashionable and practical was an ice house, where ice blocks could be stored and brought into the kitchens as needed. A statue of Dick Whittington facing St Albans rather than London, was standing on top of it in the 1930s.

Dr Alexander von Mayersbach was in possession of the estate by 1790 when it was sold to John Samuel Torriano, a major in the East India Company's Service. From 1796 it was held in trust for Arthur Ormsby and from 1823 for Charles Poole. Later The Grove was part of the Marquess of Abercorn's estate and was sold to John Webb in 1861.

Mrs Eliza Brightwen (1830-1906) was the most popular naturalist of her day.[2] She was originally a Miss Elder and married a banker, George

*93. The Grove as remodelled for the Brightwens by the architect, Brightwen Binyon.*

Brightwen, in 1855. They came to The Grove about 1872 and employed Brightwen Binyon to remodel the house, which he did by giving it bay windows and gables in the Norman Shaw manner. She made the house and grounds a wildlife sanctuary, allowing red squirrels to come and take sugar from the dining room table and birds to sit on the rim of her cup. Rare animals like an Indian mongoose and a South African antelope lived for a time in the grounds and lemurs and an Egyptian jerboa had the run of the conservatory. She gave the animals and birds names and drew them in natural poses but with slightly fanciful captions such as 'Jack sunneth himself' and 'He disdaineth the fair sex'. She used her drawings to illustrate her books, *Wild Nature won by Kindness* and *Quiet Hours with Nature*. Nonetheless she was a practical naturalist. She made a collection of birds' skulls, obtained by boiling and bleaching the heads of dead birds which were brought to her. The collection was deposited in the St Albans Museum.

Her interest in plants led on to horticulture and she grew rare specimens in her conservatory and unusual trees were planted in the grounds. She supplied the London hospitals with flowers from the grounds throughout the summer months and parties from the East End were welcomed each year and entertained at Grove Farm. She had been widowed in 1883 and died herself in 1906, when the property was put up for sale. Her nephew, Sir Edmund Gosse, edited her autobiography published in 1909.

Sir Edward Cassel bought The Grove for his daughter. She was married to Wilfred Ashley, later Lord Mount Temple, who as Minister of Transport 1924-9, introduced roundabouts for roads. They were the parents of Edwina Mountbatten. GEC took over The Grove in 1949 and it became Marconi Space and Defence Systems Ltd. The house was demolished in 1979, but Marconi remain on site.

## LIMES HOUSE[3]

The building now called Limes House appears on Henry Sayer's 1827 map, when it was owned by Thomas Sharp Smith. It seems to have continued in the possession of the Smith family until at least 1917, although none of them ever seem to have lived there and it was always occupied by tenants.

94.  *The library at The Grove.*

95.  *Mrs Brightwen's drawings of her tame jackdaw.*

96.  *The gourd pergola at The Grove, where the warted gourd, custard gourd and other exotica were grown.*

*97. Mrs Brightwen with her nephew, the poet Edmund Gosse, and his family.*

The house was extended after 1864 to the plans of R.L. Roumieu who was designing houses in Harrow Weald at about the same time. It was then known as The Limes.  George Donaldson, an art dealer with a gallery in Bond Street, lived there from 1891-96.  He was a benefactor of the Victoria & Albert Museum and the Royal College and Royal Academy of Music.  The house became known as Lymes Holme from 1897-1935, and then Limes House.  Sir Frederick Handley Page (1815-1962) lived there from 1922 until his death.  He was an aircraft designer and manufacturer and produced air-liners and, for the RAF, bombers between the two World Wars.  His executors sold the house in 1969 to become The Limes Country Club, which flourished for several years.  In 1995 planning permission was granted for it to become a Care Home, but in January 1998 the house was being restored to its former glory and two sympathetically designed apartment blocks were nearing completion.

98. *Limes House was sometimes known as The Limes. The house probably dates from the early 19th century, but was extended after 1864 to the designs of R.L. Roumieu.*

99. *A scene in the grounds of Limes House.*

# Houses on Stanmore Hill

## HILL HOUSE

Hill House[1] at the top of Stanmore Hill is a high quality building dating from some time before 1771, with a parapet in the centre of two pedimented wings. The coach house and stables are alongside. It has had at least three names: the Great House from 1771 until the 1820s, when it became the Mansion House, and Hill House from 1899. The first known owner was John Boys, vicar of Redbourn, Hertfordshire, who also owned Aylwards just below it and Broomfield, the next house up the hill. It is possible that he had carved the site of Hill House and its pleasure grounds out of his swathe of land on Stanmore Hill and had built the house himself. He sold the Great House in 1771 to the Revd Samuel Parr of Harrow School, who had been thwarted in his desire to become headmaster of Harrow after the

*100.  Hill House built before 1771, possibly by the Boys family, who owned land all around.*

*101.  The Rev. Samuel Parr who opened a school at Hill House in a fit of pique, having been passed over for the headship of Harrow School.*

death of Robert Carey Sumner in that year. Parr borrowed money from Sumner's brother, William, to effect the purchase and brought with him from Harrow forty pupils and an assistant master, the Revd David Roderick. The greenhouse was converted into a schoolroom and other outbuildings were made into a playroom and studies and the school officially opened on 14 October 1771.

The memoirs of one of the pupils, Thomas Maurice, who became assistant keeper at the British Museum, suggest that they enjoyed a good deal of freedom and were able to become involved in escapades 'at a certain taberna, then existing at the bottom of Stanmore Hill yclept the Queen's Head'. Another boy drowned by falling through the ice on a pond opposite the house, presumably the Spring Pond. Although sometimes severe, generally speaking Mr Parr was popular with the boys, perhaps because he loved athletic sports and encouraged the playing of cricket on the bowling green on the common. This suggests that the bowling green was no longer kept up as such, for surely cricket would have damaged the turf. But when the first generation of boys had passed through his hands the school failed and he left the Great House empty to go on to Colchester Grammar School in 1777. He became headmaster of Norwich School in 1779, by which time he seems to

have been making enough money to pay off his debt to William Sumner. Being in full possession of the house in 1780, he sold it to John Hume of Queen Street, Westminster. Samuel Parr then settled at Hatton, Warwickshire as Perpetual Curate and a memoir, his sermons and correspondence were published by Johnstone John in 1828.

John Hume seems to have let the house and it was occupied by James Savage in 1811 when Hume died, leaving it in the hands of trustees. John Sharpe of Leamington bought it in 1824 and leased it to the Revd John Augustus Barron two years later, to turn it into a school again. This school prospered and Barron finally bought the house from Sharpe's trustees in 1842. He sent his pupils to church at Harrow Weald because he was not satisfied with the preaching of the aged Mr Chauvel, rector of Great Stanmore.

Ten years later the house's most famous occupant took possession, Charles Drury Edward Fortnum, son of the founder of Fortnum and Mason's. He had a collection of classical and renaissance bronzes and statuary which he left to the Ashmolean Museum at Oxford and 800 rings also given to Oxford. He had already presented two rings of special interest to Queen Victoria at the time of her Golden Jubilee in 1887. One, a diamond signet, had belonged to Henrietta Maria, queen of Charles I and

*102. Broomfield was a mid-19th century house designed by James Knowles. It stood on the site of an earlier house owned by the Boys family.*

103. *The Woodlands was the home of Lord Halsbury, Lord Chancellor of Great Britain. He died in 1921 and is buried in St John's churchyard.*

the other was a golden sapphire signet of Queen Mary, the wife of William III. Mr Fortnum died in 1899, only a month before his wife, and Hill House became a further endowment for the University of Oxford. Charles Hickson Waterlow leased it from the university for 21 years from 1899. The house has now been converted into flats.

Waterlow's lease[2] shows that there were four bedrooms and a dressing room on the upper floor; four bedrooms, WC, bathroom, linen room, three servants' rooms and a back landing on the first floor; a hall, bay morning room, dining room, lobby and WC, two bedrooms, drawing room, library, small drawing room, dining room, conservatory and store room on the ground floor. Connected by a passage were the offices, scullery, kitchen, housekeeper's room, butler's pantry, basement, yard, furnace room, servants' WC, coal cellar, stables, loft, harness room, coach house, coach room and stable yard. No wonder it could be converted into flats.

Across Stanmore Hill surrounded by a curved red-brick wall stood the farmyard and outbuildings, divided from what was probably a kitchen garden by another brick wall. They are built on the edge of Little Common. As a bricked up doorway in the wall onto Stanmore Hill exactly matches in style the similarly blocked door into the garden and pleasure grounds of Hill House, it is fairly safe to assume

that the farm and walled garden formed part of the property from earliest days. A plan[3] dating from the period of John Sharpe's ownership shows a cottage and outbuildings, which are now (1998) known as Rose Cottage and Summerlands.

## BROOMFIELD
Next to Hill House on the top side was a mid-19th century house designed by James Knowles. It was a handsome brick house with projecting bays and a central veranda, opening onto a terrace above a sunken lawn. A modern house rather confusingly called Broomfield House now stands on the site. However, a plan[4] of the late 1820s shows an earlier house belonging to Edward Boys, grandson of the Revd John Boys of Redbourn.

## WOODLANDS
Miss Catherine Martin lived at Woodlands in the 1830s and 40s. She was very well known locally because of her kindness to the poor and her benefactions, such as her endowment of the Infants' School. The Earl of Halsbury, the Lord Chancellor who was nationally known, lived there from 1885. The *Times* rather pompously announced his comings and goings: 'The Lord Chancellor arrived in town yester-

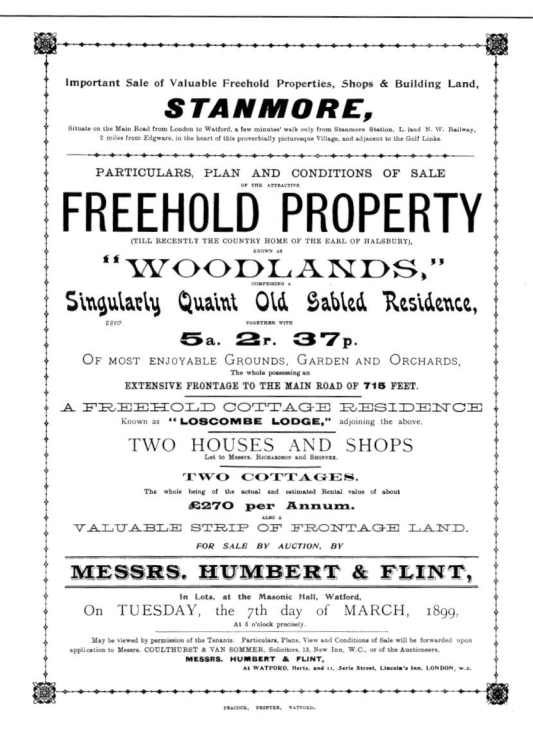

104. *Sales brochure for the Woodlands estate, 1899.*

105. *Robins Hill is noted for the fact that Edward Wilson, who died during Scott's Antarctic expedition, lived here from 1899 to 1901, while studying for his medical degree. He formed a friendship with Mrs Brightwen because of their similar interests. The earlier name of the house was Loscombe Lodge, after the family who owned it before 1853.*

106. *Nunlands is a pleasant early 18th-century house, now offices.*

day morning from Woodlands, Stanmore. His Lordship was engaged for some considerable time in the transaction of official business at the House of Lords, after which he returned to the country. He will again return to town tomorrow morning.' (Jan 1885.) The *Harrow Observer* of 1899 carried the interesting intelligence that 'Lady Halsbury, who is the second wife of the Lord Chancellor, is extremely fond of travelling and of country life. In consequence she is seldom seen in society, though she is, of course, present at all the great political parties of the year. Lady Halsbury has two children, a son and a daughter.' Halsbury Close is now on the site of Woodlands.

When the Halsburys put Woodlands (not to be confused with the other house called Woodlands in Clamp Hill) up for sale in 1899, the five-acre estate included some cottages and shops near the junction with Green Lane and Loscombe Lodge, a charming eighteenth-century 'cottage residence' that is now known as Robins Hill. Loscombe Lodge was home from 1899 to 1901 to Edward Wilson, the naturalist who lost his life on Scott's Antarctic Expedition. Charles Wintringham Loscombe, from whom the house takes its name, owned the whole Woodlands estate prior to 1853.[5]

# Two Great Houses

After Canons, Bentley Priory and Stanmore Park were the two great houses of Stanmore in the eighteenth and nineteenth centuries and both came into the hands of the Royal Air Force between the two World Wars. Although the Priory was actually situated across the parish boundary in Harrow Weald a portion of the estate lay in Stanmore and residents, like the Marquess of Abercorn, attended Great Stanmore church and buried their dead there, rather than at the parish church of Harrow-on-the-Hill. All Saints Church, Harrow Weald, was not built until 1845 and the new parish was carved out of Harrow-on-the-Hill.

## BENTLEY PRIORY

A priory dependent upon St Gregory's, the house of Augustinian Canons at Canterbury, seems to have been established at Bentley in the early thirteenth century, although relatively little is known about it. Matthew Paris's Chronicle for the year 1248 describes 'the miserable death of the prior of Benethly' who had been accidentally suffocated when a rick of wheat whose value he had been estimating, tottered and fell upon him.[1] The Harrow court rolls for 1512 suggest that the priors had in the past provided a priest to say mass in the priory chapel for the people round about, but that there had been no prior for twenty years past and no priest to say mass for two years.[2] After the dissolution of the monasteries the priory was in the hands of the Colte family from 1546 to c1640 and then the Coghills and relatives until 1761. During the next few years there were several sales and consolidation of surrounding land and an estate in Harrow and Great Stanmore was sold to James Duberly, an army contractor, in 1775.[3]

*107. (left)  Priory House where early foundations have been discovered, which perhaps relate to the medieval priory.*

*108. (above)  Bentley Priory at the time of Queen Adelaide's residence, from the south.*

## THE DASHING MARQUESS OF ABERCORN

The medieval priory buildings were probably near Priory House in Clamp Hill, where old foundations have been found.[4] James Duberly built a new house and then sold the estate to James Hamilton, later 1st Marquess of Abercorn, in 1788. For the next ten years Sir John Soane was engaged in altering and adding to Duberly's house. Plans and drawings are preserved at the Soane Museum. The house featured a circular tribune beyond the hall where works of art could be shown to advantage. Lysons approved, for he called it 'a noble mansion, in which convenience is united with magnificence'.

The Marquess (1756-1817) was a colourful personality, dubbed Don Whiskerandos by Richard Brinsley Sheridan and described by another contemporary as 'tall, erect and muscular, with an air of grace and dignity, dark complexion, more like a Spaniard than an Englishman'. He married three times, divorcing his second wife who eloped with, and subsequently married his first wife's younger brother. He was always to be seen surrounded by a bevy of young beauties clad in the scantiest of clothing (in classical style) at assemblies and was known as something of a roué. The most distinguished social, political and artistic company was entertained at Bentley Priory during his time. The Princess of Wales, the exiled King of Sweden, Pitt, Canning, Lord Liverpool all came, rubbing shoulders with theatricals like Kemble and Mrs Siddons and with Lady Hamilton, Lord Nelson's mistress. Sir Walter Scott revised the proofs for *Marmion* while sitting in the summerhouse on the island in the middle of the lake.

The house was extended between 1810-18 by the architect, Robert Smirke, which may account for Brewer's dismissal of it in his *Beauties of England & Wales* as 'an irregular range of brick building, destitute of architectural beauty, and of rather a gloomy character'. Lady Morgan, a frequent visitor wrote 'the house is no house at all, for it looks like a little town, which you will believe when I tell you that 120 people slept under the roof during the Christmas holidays without including the underservants'.

The first Marchioness had died of consumption and all six of her children suffered the same fate, although two, the eldest son, Lord Hamilton and the second daughter, Catherine lived to be 28 and both married and had children. Catherine's husband was Lord Aberdeen, who after her death in 1812 was persuaded by Lord Castlereagh to be British plenipotentiary at Vienna in the final struggles of the Napoleonic Wars. He married Lord Hamilton's widow in 1816 as his second wife, becoming both uncle and step-father to her children. The young Lord Hamilton succeeded to his grandfather's title in 1817 and subsequently became the first Duke of Abercorn in 1868. Lord Aberdeen's children by his first wife died of consumption like their mother and a daughter of his second marriage died at the age of 15. Her mother only lived to be 42. No wonder Lord Aberdeen is considered a serious and rather sombre figure. He was twice Foreign Secretary 1828-30 and 1841-46 and Prime Minister from 1852-55. One of the four children who did survive him became rector of Great Stanmore in 1848.

The 1st Marquess purchased the estate in small detached pieces as opportunity offered and threw them into the park and pleasure grounds. The 2nd Marquess enlarged the estate by buying Stanmore Park from the Drummond family in 1839;[5] the lordship of the manor from the Duke of Buckingham and Chandos in 1840;[6] and Aylwards from

*109. Queen Adelaide.*

John Marks's widow and children in 1843.[7] He left Bentley Priory in the early 1840s, according to his son, out of self preservation, as the house was set in such beautiful surroundings and so close to London that friends having once arrived refused to move. His wife is remembered for a cordial known as 'Her Grace's bottle', which she used to distribute among the poor and frail of Stanmore. It was based upon old whisky with a few other things added and was immensely popular.

## QUEEN ADELAIDE

A very distinguished tenant moved into Bentley Priory in 1848, Queen Adelaide, widow of William IV. She was nearing the end of her life and indeed lived for little more than a year and a half, having been advised to move to Stanmore for the 'salubrious air'. Queen Victoria and Prince Albert visited her in November 1848, combining it with a trip to Harrow School. Queen Adelaide attended divine service at the old church during her sojourn in Stanmore and took an interest in the new one, attending the laying of the foundation stone by Lord Aberdeen in March 1849. By the time of her death at the Priory on 2 December 1849, the Marquess of Abercorn was on the brink of finan-cial ruin, having debts of more than £400,000 at Coutts's bank. He saved himself by a series of sales. He had already sold Stanmore Park to Mr George Carr Glyn in 1848. Bentley Priory and its parkland were purchased by Sir John Kelk, the railway engineer in 1852[8] and farmland south of Stanmore Park, including Old Church Farm was sold to St Bartholomew's Hospital in 1856.[9]

## SIR JOHN KELK

Kelk discovered that some parts of the land were encumbered with annuities and although he took possession of the estate in 1853, the actual deed of sale was not drawn up until 1857,[10] when the problems had been resolved. Sir John built the clock tower which today is such a distinguishing feature of Bentley Priory when seen from a distant viewing point such as Belmont, and remodelled the interior on Italianate lines. He sold it to Frederick Gordon of Bloomsbury Square for £75,000 in 1881.[11] The Sale Particulars advertised the woodlands and plantations as well adapted for rearing of game and especially for preserving pheasants. The estate buildings included a gamekeeper's house. The bailiff's house stood in Clamp Hill. The Home Farm with model farm buildings was in the park close by and there

*110. Bentley Priory from the north east. The clock tower which makes the building such a landmark was added by Sir John Kelk, the railway engineer who owned the estate for thirty years from 1852.*

were cottages for the dairyman and carpenter. There were two lodges on Common Road, three in Clamp Hill and the Church Lodge, opposite the church and still standing at the corner of Old Lodge Way. An orangery adorned the upper part of the grounds and there was a deer park. That tradition continues as there is still a deer park in Heriots Wood, though in a different position. The brochure artfully suggested that 200 acres could well be built over without damaging the surroundings of the house!

## BENTLEY PRIORY AS A HOTEL

Mr Gordon already owned several hotels (*see p132*) and turned Bentley Priory to the same use in 1885, running a four-in-hand coach from London to bring guests out for a day in the country. He made much of the royal connection, with Queen Adelaide's summerhouse figuring in the hotel brochure and perhaps created the room known today

*111. (below) The recently restored staircase at Bentley Priory.*

*112. (right) The vestibule designed by Soane, photographed in 1945.*

113. *Lower Priory Farm, Clamp Hill, the farm of Bentley Priory.*

115. *One of the lodges of Bentley Priory. This one with its heavily carved barge boards stands on the corner of Uxbridge Road and Old Lodge Way. The Abercorn coat-of-arms on the gable suggests that the lodge was built before the estate was sold to Sir John Kelk in 1852.*

114. *The Summerhouse Lake, which is now a nature reserve, with Bentley Priory on the hill above. Walter Scott is said to have worked on* **Marmion** *while sitting in the summerhouse, probably a predecessor of the one seen here. The last summerhouse was destroyed by fire in the early 1990s.*

116.  *Bentley Priory became a girls' school in 1908.  This is the lecture hall with seating for 48 girls.*

117.  *An art class in progress in the school's studio.*

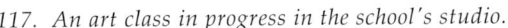

as the Adelaide Room, after turning her actual living quarters into the kitchen and service area.[12] The brochure of 1885 shows a well appointed hotel with a grand staircase, halls, dining-rooms, library and salons of 'sumptuous character'. The circular music room, presumably Soane's work, was said to be formed after the model of the tribune in the Uffizi Palace. Pictures in the brochure and in the *Illustrated London News* show the Grand Conservatory or Winter Garden, a shady avenue of trees, an Italian Garden, Cedar Garden, the lake and other delightful prospects.[13]

Although Mr Gordon was instrumental in bringing the railway from Wealdstone to Stanmore in 1890, to make the hotel easier of access to guests, the venture was never a financial success and it seems to have been his family home again by 1891. He died in 1904 and Bentley Priory and the house became a private school for young ladies from 1908 until 1924 or 5. The Air Ministry purchased the house and forty acres of the grounds in 1926 for about £25,000. (For the history of Frederick Gordon's other estates in Stanmore see pp130-134).

## HODGKINS

Andrew Drummond (1688-1769), the young son of Sir John Drummond, came to London from Scotland about 1712, or possibly a few years earlier. He established himself as a goldsmith and started

banking on the east side of Charing Cross at the sign of the Golden Eagle in 1717, moving to the present site of Drummonds Bank (now the Drummond Branch of the Royal Bank of Scotland) in 1760. Among his clients was the 1st Duke of Chandos. Perhaps for this reason he bought a house called Hodgkins in Great Stanmore in 1729 and having created a broad estate over the years, built a mansion to do it justice, in 1763.

Hodgkins[14] with its barns, stables, gardens and orchards, was a copyhold messuage, first mentioned in the court rolls of Great Stanmore in 1670, when Henry Pettit of Pynnacles was the owner. It stood on the south side of Colliers Lane, more or less on the site of the later mansion. (Colliers Lane was diverted to run north of the church about 1800 and the remaining eastern portion is now named Rectory Lane.) The Duke of Chandos granted Drummond a parcel of the waste in 1741, with sixteen large elms standing before his courtyard and outhouses and 47 small elms and 32 limes standing in two rows along his garden wall for one shilling a year. This must be the avenue of trees shown on Rocque's 1754 map of Middlesex and on Milne's land use map of 1800 leading to Belmont (now part of Stanmore golf course). Under the terms of the grant neither the Duke nor Mr Drummond were to cut down any of the trees and should any die or decay Drummond or his heirs were to plant new ones. In 1745 Andrew Drummond bought the fourteen-acre meadowland

*118. Stanmore Park, an engraving by J.P. Neale in 1816. The drawing shows the back of the house and the additional storey at the rear. Compare this with illustration 121, which shows the front view.*

119.  *A painting by Zoffany of the Drummond family at Stanmore Park.  Andrew Drummond who had died in 1769, before this work was executed, sits in the centre with his dog.  From the left, Andrew's grandson, John sits on a pony attended by a groom;  Andrew's son, John, stands in front of his own daughter, Jane who is mounted on a horse.  To the right of Andrew sits his daughter-in-law, Charlotte, his granddaughter, Charlotte and his grandson, George.  The house can be seen in the background.*

of the head tenement, Sym Rookes, and in 1749, the site of another head tenement, Buggs, on the north side of Colliers Lane; and when Joseph Taylor, a gentleman who owned much of the land surrounding Hodgkins, died in 1760, Drummond acquired all of it, becoming owner of the lands that had once belonged to Buggs, Brookfield, Thrums Mead, Cock Allens, Fitchels, another messuage and twenty acres in the common fields.

## STANMORE PARK

The aged Andrew Drummond ordered the building of a new house in 1763 and created a park around it out of this meadowland. He employed the well-known architect John Vardy who had been working on Spencer House, St James's Place for the past few years, where he had created a magnificent Palladian set-piece in the famous Palm Room. Vardy designed Stanmore Park, but after

*120. George Harley Drummond (1783-1855), the man who lost most of his money at play and had to mortgage Stanmore Park and retire to Scotland.*

121. *William Ellis drew the southern aspect of Stanmore Park in 1806, showing its proximity to the brick church. The water is actually an ornamental lake, not a canal. Watercolours of the period show it with a temple at the east end. The centre portion of the house had had a storey added.*

his death in 1765, it was completed by Sir William Chambers. Drummond's wife, Isabella, was long since dead, having been buried at Great Stanmore in February 1731, a week or two after the birth and death of her son, Andrew. An older son, John, born in 1723, before the move to Stanmore, and two other boys survived to inherit the bank. Following Andrew Drummond's death at the age of 81 in 1769, John (1723-74) raised the roof and made other alterations to the garden front of the house.[15]

Several paintings were made at Stanmore by Zoffany.[16] That of John and his family (*ill. 119*), was set in the grounds, and rather oddly includes Andrew who was already dead, sitting on a bench beside his daughter-in-law, Charlotte. The scene is set on the top of a hill, possibly Belmont which had come into the estate, and the house can be discerned faintly in the distance. Tradition has it that Zoffany's *Beggars on the road to Stanmore* (*ill. 122*) is based upon a group seen by the artist while travelling to undertake this commission. John's son, George (1758-89) who was charmingly portrayed by Gainsborough, left the estate heavily encumbered with debt and his son, George Harley Drummond (1783-1855) is supposed to have gambled away £20,000 in a single night at White's Club, lost to Beau Brummell. He is also reputed to have won at play against Lord Grosvenor and to have turned down the offer of Belgravia, which was then a snipe bog, in lieu of £40,000. He was obliged to leave the bank because of his losses and retired to Drumtochty in Scotland. Stanmore Park was let to the Countess of Aylesford in 1815 and the estate was mortgaged to Alexander Munro in 1820. Lord Castlereagh, the unpopular and unfortunate Foreign Secretary, also stayed there for a time before his death in 1822.

## ABERCORN AND WOLVERTON

The Marquess of Abercorn of Bentley Priory purchased the estate in 1839 and let it to the Earl of Wicklow who had family connections through marriage. The Stanmore Tithe Award shows that the estate was then divided into the 87-acre South Park stretching from the Temple pond to Belmont and North Park on the other side of Uxbridge Road, 66 acres including Boot Pond. Old Church Farm and Park Farm at the northern end of the avenue of trees were also part of it. When all the Stanmore estates of the Marquess were auctioned in 1848, Stanmore Park was Lot 2. There were then 1270 acres within a ring fence and another 130 acres outside. The Home Farm, known as Park Farm was described as the most spacious in the county.[17]

122.  'Beggars on the road to Stanmore' by Zoffany.

*123. By 1884 bay windows had been added to the dining and drawing rooms of Stanmore Park and the interior had been altered. The stable block can be seen on the right, built on land purchased by Andrew Drummond in 1763 from James Dalton, the rector.*

George Carr Glyn, partner in Glyn, Mills, Currie & Company bank, bought it. He became Lord Wolverton in 1869 and was chairman of the London and North-Western Railway. His son, a personal friend of Gladstone, and Postmaster General, followed him as owner of Stanmore Park, until his death in 1887, but the house and farm were sometimes let, as in February 1881, when they were advertised in the *Watford Observer*. Frederick Gordon of Bentley Priory purchased Stanmore Park in 1887.

## LAST DAYS

Stanmore Park ended its days as a preparatory school belonging to Mr Kemball Cook, which moved from Brighton at the end of the 1880s and went on to Hertford in 1937. The Revd Vernon Royle, a fine England cricketer, ran the school from 1900, when H. Kemball-Cook esq. left the area, the auction sale of his furniture being advertised in the *Harrow Observer* in December of that year. The house and grounds were acquired by the RAF in the spring of 1938 and the house was bulldozed to make way for hutments to house RAF personnel in June. There had been no consultation whatsoever with the local council or populace.

# Growing Villages

## VESTRY AFFAIRS

The manor courts of Great Stanmore continued to be recorded until 1936 and those of Little Stanmore until 1924, but the bulk of the work from the seventeenth century onward dealt with exchanges of land and property and had little to do with local government. In most parishes the vestry, a regular meeting of prominent parishioners meeting in the vestry of the parish church to discuss church matters, became more powerful following the passing of the 1601 Poor Law Act which made it responsible for the care of the poor. The power of the manor courts was largely superseded as other vestry officials like the Surveyors of Highways took over the maintenance of roads. Presumably both the Stanmore parishes had vestries with churchwardens in earlier times, but the earliest surviving records are a surveyor of highways book from Little Stanmore commencing in 1654 and a vestry order book of 1730 from Great Stanmore. These and extant overseers' and churchwardens' accounts provide a picture of everyday life in Stanmore for the humbler part of the population during the eighteenth and nineteenth centuries.

The vestry itself was run by greater landowners or tenants, often presided over by the incumbent

125. *The Crown on Church Road, another venue for vestry meetings. The 18th-century building shown here was replaced in the 1930s by the present building.*

of the parish. William Hallett and his successors at Canons appeared at Little Stanmore Vestry and Andrew Drummond and Thomas Clutterbuck at Great Stanmore. Seven or eight people usually attended, but numbers grew to fifteen in Great Stanmore in the nineteenth century. Meetings

124. *The Queen's Head, a venue for vestry meetings, originally stood on the other side of Church Road. It was in existence by 1714.*

*126. A photograph of the Wealdstone and Stanmore police force taken at Stanmore.*

were held in various places, some a great deal more comfortable than the vestry rooms. The Queen's Head, the Crown and the Abercorn Arms provided hospitality in Great Stanmore and the Crane (later the Chandos Arms) in Little Stanmore. Great Stanmore sometimes used a room at the workhouse from 1789 to 1835 and later the new schoolroom on Stanmore Hill.

## CONSTABLES AND BEADLES

The constable and headborough (deputy constable) continued to be nominated by the manor court at Great Stanmore until 1805, though both these officials were named by the vestry at Little Stanmore from 1668. After the Sturges Bourne Vestries Act 1818 justices selected the constables from short-lists drawn up by vestries. The constable had administrative duties in addition to maintaining law and order. He was responsible for executing Justices' warrants, collecting national taxes and relieving or removing itinerant vagrants, depending upon whether the beggars had passes or not. He also dealt with matters concerning the militia.

The Great Stanmore constable in 1828, Francis Chapman, was assisted by four headboroughs.[1] Perhaps there was hooliganism in the area for the vestry decided the following year, to have notices printed 'cautioning the boys in this parish from assembling in the town to the annoyance of the public and in breach of the public peace'. A beadle was appointed in 1834 at a weekly wage of seven shillings to be paid out of the church rate: 'Such Beadle to be employed about the village in keeping order prosecuting vagrancy and enforcing an obedience to the laws by the keepers of beer shops and preventing disorder particularly on the Sabbath day'. Much more terrible crimes were perpetrated. On 2 September 1829 it was resolved 'that the vestry feel it as their bounden duty to take the prosecution of a man charged with the rape of a child about four years and a quarter old on Mr Drummond's premises, into their hands and for that purpose do authorise the vestry clerk to conduct such prosecution'.

Miscreants could be placed in the parish stocks which were first mentioned in 1639 and were moved to the workhouse yard in 1819. The cage for imprisoning offenders, built in 1791, was also at the workhouse in Great Stanmore. Not surprisingly Little Stanmore and Edgware joined forces to erect a cage in 1767, but Edgware did not pay its share of the cost until 1780. Although the Stanmores became part of the Metropolitan Police District in 1842, parish constables and headboroughs continued to be appointed into the 1860s.

127.  *The Abercorn Arms in Stanmore Hill is an 18th-century building with a later addition.  Its proudest moment was in 1814 when it was the scene of a meeting between the Prince Regent and Louis XVIII of France who had been spending his exile at Hartwell, Bucks. As this print of c1846 shows, the hotel was a regular stopping place for the London-Watford coach.*

## THE COURT HOUSE[2]

The Stanmores were in the Gore petty-sessional division of the Middlesex Commission Area. From 1551 courts were mostly held in the village of Edgware in a room in one or other of the many inns. The Crane, later called the Chandos Arms, on the Little Stanmore side of Watling Street and the Abercorn Arms on Stanmore Hill were among the places used in the eighteenth century. A house next to the Chandos Arms belonging to the brewer, Thomas Clutterbuck, and joined to the inn by cellars and passageways, became the first proper court house in 1850 (*see ill. 129*). It was in use until 1913 (still lit only by candles on gloomy days) when it was replaced by a new court house at the Hyde, Hendon.

## SURVEYORS OF HIGHWAYS

Parishes, as opposed to manors, were first made responsible for highways in 1555. Surveyors had to be appointed to decide what repairs needed to be done and to organise and supervise them. In practice local Justices made the appointment from lists of names drawn up by the churchwardens and vestry. All parishioners who owned either a plough or arable land were obliged to supply a cart for the work for four days (six after 1691)

*128. This print is labelled 'Stanmore Toll-house' and describes the building as 'one of the handsomest near London'. The cupola housed a lantern 'an important mark to travellers on dark nights'. It was probably one of the new toll-houses erected after several turnpike trusts around London were consolidated into the Metropolis Roads in 1826. It stood near the top of Stanmore Hill, oppposite the Vine.*

*129.  The Chandos Arms in Edgware High Street and to the right the court house, formerly a building belonging, like the pub next door, to the brewer, Thomas Clutterbuck.  It was used as a court house from 1850 to 1913.*

each year.  Able-bodied householders had to labour on the roads for the same number of days, but a payment could be made instead or a substitute provided.

The Little Stanmore surveyors had an onerous job with such a heavily used road as Watling Street in their care.  The main Stanmore roads were turnpiked in the eighteenth century and came under the Metropolis Roads Commission set up in 1826 to consolidate fourteen separate trusts operating in the metropolitan area north of the Thames.  A toll house stood opposite the Vine on Stanmore Hill, on the Watford road and another at the bottom end of Edgware High Street.  The vestry made representation in 1829 about the state of the road and footpath in the village which had been made dangerous by the placing of several large gratings (presumably for drainage) which had caused accidents.[3]

## OVERSEERS OF THE POOR

There were usually two overseers of the poor in each parish, but ten were chosen in Great Stanmore in 1828.  Poor rates were levied on the value of property and varied in number and amount from year to year as need arose.  Sixpence in the pound was a common levy in the eighteenth century, but it rose to one shilling in 1806 when the price of corn and consequently bread was high.  Money for licences granted at the manor courts allowing encroachments upon the common, was added to the poor account in Great Stanmore at the turn of the nineteenth century, when a series of bad harvests and the trials and tribulations of the revolutionary wars with France were causing special hardship.

The recipients of parish relief fall into several categories:  the aged poor unable to labour;  the chronic sick who were generally unfit for work;  those sick for short periods;  widowed and deserted mothers of young children;  unmarried mothers;  orphans;  able-bodied poor who were unemployed and passing vagrants.

*130. The Lake Almshouses near St Lawrence's in Whitchurch Lane, maintained by a charitable fund established by Sir Lancelot Lake under the will of his mother, dated 1646. This picture taken c1915 shows some of the inhabitants.*

## HOUSES FOR THE POOR

Parish houses were maintained in both parishes for the aged poor and families unable to pay rent for other cottages. There were three in Little Stanmore, 'up town', 'below the turnpike' and by the Ninepin & Bowl. The one up town had a thatched roof which had to be repaired in 1758 following heavy rain which had soaked the inmates in their beds.[4] There were two cottages with gardens adjoining the churchyard in Great Stanmore.[5] The gardens were divided into allotments for the inmates in 1783. These cottages were sold in 1787 preparatory to a workhouse being built on Stanmore Hill in 1788. Although these parish houses were places of shelter rather than workhouses, it is clear that work was sometimes provided as spinning wheels were purchased for the Great Stanmore houses in 1752.

There were also the Lake Almshouses close to St Lawrence Whitchurch, which were separately maintained by a charitable fund set up by Sir Lancelot Lake under the terms of his mother's will of 1646. They were intended to house four old men and three old women who should be regular in church attendance and unmarried.

Henry Hooper gave a group of cottages near the junction of Green Lane and Stanmore Hill for the use of poor widows in 1850. They were not endowed and were apparently in a dreadful state by the end of the century, no repairs having been undertaken in the meantime. The Medical Officer of Health advised that they should be condemned

in 1903 and stated that the only reason that he had not done so before was his fear that the inmates would be left with no alternative but the workhouse. The Rector rather defensively replied that money would have been forthcoming to put the almshouses into good order, but that there was no way that a through draught and modern requirements could be met.[6]

## WEEKLY PENSIONERS[7]

Weekly sums were allocated to the needy. Rebecca Howard was granted three shillings a week towards the support of her two children during her husband's absence in May 1779. If a man was away serving in the Militia, provision could legally be made for his family. George Pepler was substituting for someone else in the Militia in 1782 and the vestry needed to know for whom before making an allowance to his wife. A man in Little Stanmore was extraordinarily fortunate in 1810, being granted sixteen weeks' pension in advance to enable him to undertake a seabathing cure!

## DISCRETIONARY PAYMENTS[8]

In addition to money payments, help was given in kind. Widow Brown's children were supplied with shoes in May 1779, but alas in July 1781 the vestry clerk noted that Widow Brown had recently married John Elliot and that they had both deserted her four children who were left to the care of the parish. Items of clothing and food and fuel were frequently given.

## LOOKING AFTER CHILDREN[9]

Normally young children were fostered and older ones apprenticed. John Gold, Mrs Darnell, Mrs Rogers and Davies regularly fostered children in the 1780s, receiving 2s 6d per week per child. Davies was being paid 1s 6d per week to care for the bastard child 'begotten on the body of the said Davies's daughter' in 1779 and five years later was receiving the same sum for the support of 'Hamilton's bastard child'. Whether or not this was the same child is not clear.

The birth of an illegitimate child caused a good deal of expense to the parish. Ilezia Darnell in the late stages of pregnancy was taken before the magistrates on the 6 and 8 April 1784 to swear as to the name of the father of her forthcoming child. The costs of travel and her examination and oath amounted to nine shillings. A warrant for the arrest of Robert Buckingham whom she had named and other expenses attending his apprehension came to 3s 3d. Ilezia was given 2s 6d on the 22nd April and five shillings on the 24th when she was in labour. She was given further sums, three shillings on the 28th April, the 4th May, 10th May and four shillings on the 21st May. The christening of the baby and churching of the mother on the 22nd May cost another 1s 9d. Thereafter Mrs Darnell (perhaps the baby's grandmother and the foster mother mentioned above) received 2s 6d per week. In this instance the father did indemnify the parish to the tune of £10, but all too often the fathers simply disappeared.

## APPRENTICESHIP[10]

Burrell's daughters seem to have been sent into service in London at a Mrs Bartlett's in 1784. The eldest came home from service in March and received one shilling. She went back in May, having her coach hire paid and a month later the younger came home. There are no records of girls being regularly apprenticed to a trade, but a number of boys were indentured. 16-year-old John Burch was bound to William Payne of Chesham, Bucks, a cordwainer, at an assignment fee of £25 in 1802 and Thomas Carter aged 15 was apprenticed to a local baker, Thomas Spence, in 1822. The overseers and justices who signed the papers inquired into the character and circumstances of the baker before binding the boy. Both these boys were relatively old at the start of their apprenticeship and were bound until the age of 21. Prior to an act of parliament of 1768, parish children or the children of men receiving poor relief had been bound until the age of 24, a form of slavery.

## THE SICK POOR[11]

Poor women in the parish were paid to nurse others and a doctor was retained. The bill of a surgeon, Mr Andrews, in 1782 was £10 16s 6d and he was 'to continue to attend the Poor and provide and administer such medicines as necessary' for eight guineas half yearly. Andrews had taken over the former Assembly Rooms in Stanmore. A Mrs Stone was paid half a guinea for delivering Hearne's wife in 1783. Often the sick person died. Mary Street was ill in March 1784 and receiving help from the parish. She died about the 6th April and 14 shillings was paid for her coffin and shroud and three shillings for laying her out, washing her linen and the expenses of a horse and cart. The bearers who carried her to her grave were given 5s 4d and that is the last that we hear of her.

## SETTLEMENT[12]

Non-parishioners were allowed to enter a parish provided that they brought with them a settlement certificate from their home parish showing that they could be sent back there if they became paupers. As one of the ways in which legal settlement could be established was by serving an apprenticeship in a parish, pauper children were very often bound outside their home parish. Another way was by working as a hired servant in a parish for a year and a day. Paupers were taken before the Justices to be examined as to their place of settlement.

A mother and daughter both called Mary Ford became chargeable to the parish of Great Stanmore in 1821. The mother swore on oath that she was about 70 years of age and had been born in Great Stanmore. She was single and had never married, but upwards of 39 years ago she had hired herself to Sir Thomas Whitworth of the Foundling Hospital in the parish of St Pancras, as his servant at £6 wages, board and lodging and had continued in service three years, sleeping at the Foundling Hospital where her master had apartments. Since that time she had done nothing to gain a legal settlement. She had no idea to which parish or place her father belonged, but believed that her mother at the time of her birth had belonged to Great Stanmore. Her daughter swore that she was about 43 years of age and had been born in Great Stanmore and had never done anything since her birth to gain legal settlement anywhere else. On the face of it the mother could have been removed to St Pancras and the daughter left in Stanmore. Unfortunately the records are silent as to their fate.

Mark Clarke was found to belong to Harpenden in 1829 and was to be removed there. The overseers appealed against an order of removal of Caroline Tyers and her bastard child from Watford to Stanmore a year later.

## THE WORKHOUSE[13]

A workhouse was erected on Stanmore Hill in 1788, built by Messrs Grove and Fitch within an estimate of 500 guineas. The care of the poor was normally farmed out from 1791. Thomas Bray Wiggins, cordwainer of Great Stanmore, signed a three-year contract with the churchwardens and overseers of the poor of the parish of Great Stanmore on 3 June 1816. He undertook to maintain the poor 'in a proper, convenient, wholesome and comfortable manner, maintain, lodge, clothe, keep, feed and support all the poor belonging to the parish of Great Stanmore who now are or at any time during the said term shall be in the workhouse of the said parish'. He would also relieve other poor, not in the house, as ordered by the vestry. The inmates were to have three meals a day and good and wholesome small beer. Breakfasts and suppers were to consist of bread, cheese and beer, hot broth, soup or milk. Hot dinners on Sundays, Tuesdays and Thursdays should consist of properly cooked meat and vegetables. Not above one half of the meat should be beef. The rest should be clean and wholesome. The apothecary was to decide whether salt meat would injure health and mutton and other broths were always to be available for the sick and aged poor. Clothing was to be adequate in quantity and neat in appearance. Each pauper was to have a weekday and a Sunday dress. Clean linen and stockings were to be provided every Sunday and clean sheets for the beds once a month. The children of both sexes were to be taught to read and to learn some industrious occupation. Mr Wiggins was responsible for the discipline of all the paupers, who were not allowed to go outside the workhouse without leave.

The overseers would pay him £360 per annum and he could keep the whole profit and produce arising from the labour and work of the poor within the house and five-sixths of any wages earned by paupers sent to work outside. They were only to be required to work with moderation. He had the use of the premises except for the schoolroom of the Sunday Institution and the strong room underneath called the cage.

*131. Great Stanmore Workhouse was built on the east side of Stanmore Hill below the Abercorn Arms. William Rogers, a surgeon bought it in 1838 and it became a private house. It was called the Old Place when this photograph was taken about 1930, not long before it was demolished.*

*132. Rules and Orders of Stanmore Workhouse.*

A list of rules and orders drawn up in 1820 suggest that brawling, abusive language, drunkenness, defacing walls and breaking windows were common misdemeanours. Punishments included missing meals, subsisting on bread and water, being confined in the 'dark hole' (the cage perhaps), or being sent to the House of Correction.

Mr Wiggins needed more money from the vestry in 1818 because of the large numbers out of work, but the request was refused and the vestry took over direct responsibility for the workhouse. Later contractors were John Viall of Wormley, Herts; Thomas Potter and Charles Winkley of Harrow-on-the-Hill. The amount had risen steadily from the £360 per year in 1816 to £550 in 1831, a time of agricultural depression. There were difficulties in making ends meet, let alone making a profit. Mr Winkley reported in January 1832 that he had a deficiency of £70 and upwards during the six months that he had been in charge. A week later his contract was cancelled and he was appointed master of the workhouse, receiving a weekly sum of seven shillings and maintenance for himself, his wife and three children under six. The following year economic affairs were easier and Mr Winkley again contracted to care for the poor and his salary as master ceased.

## BOUND IN UNION[14]

With the coming of the Poor Law Amendment Act of 1834 the Stanmores became part of the Hendon Union along with Edgware, Kingsbury, Harrow, Pinner and Hendon itself. John Augustus Oldham Esq and John Seabrook senior became guardians for the parish of Great Stanmore. There ensued a dreadfully unsettled period for the very poor of all seven parishes, while the Board of Guardians decided how best to exploit the Union's resources. There were four parish workhouses at Harrow, Pinner, Hendon and Stanmore. The guardians proposed in May 1835 that the aged, decayed and respectable poor should be housed at Hendon, and the lying-in women, children and unfortunate females would be at Great Stanmore; the impotent poor were to be at Pinner and the able-bodied poor at Harrow. But in August they decided that Harrow workhouse 'should be kept unoccupied for the present to ascertain if it will be required during the ensuing winter' and that the inmates should be sent to other houses. They then decreed that the poor from Stanmore should be moved to Hendon and the poor from Pinner to Stanmore, so that Pinner and Harrow workhouses could both be 'kept ready in case of an influx of able-bodied poor during the winter'. There was also a scheme for converting the Harrow house into an infirmary for the Union. All this experimentation led to much shunting of the poor around the area.

Mr Winkley was appointed master of Stanmore workhouse at a weekly salary of ten shillings and maintenance for himself and wife but only two children. His wife seems to have been working as matron at Pinner for a time. Five tons of granite were delivered and a stone-breaking yard was prepared near the engine-house and garden, where 'the men whilst at work would be free from the observation of the public and the men would be prevented from gazing at every passer-by'. The material was hard and the guardians made up the men's wages to six shillings a week, even though insufficient stone had been broken and new, stronger hammers were to be provided.

### Central Union House

The guardians eventually realised that a new central Union Workhouse was necessary and looked about for a suitable site in the autumn of 1837. Stanmore Marsh was considered, but in October 1838 a field was purchased from Mr Gares at Redhill. The contract for the building of the new house went to Mr Charles Tenter in September 1839 and it was ready in the summer of 1840.

Stanmore workhouse was sold to William Rogers, a surgeon in 1838. A new cage and engine house had to be built at the end of the Spring Pond.

# The Stanmores in Victorian Times

## GROWING NUMBERS

The population of both Great and Little Stanmore grew during the nineteenth century, from 722 and 424 respectively in 1801 to 1827 and 1069 in 1901. As the accompanying graph shows both parishes were increasing at a rapid rate until 1831. Over the next twenty years, a period typified by agricultural depression, Great Stanmore grew very slowly, increasing by only 36 people and Little Stanmore lost 65. Great Stanmore's growth during the 1850s and 60s, the golden age of farming, was marked, as was Little Stanmore's in the 1850s, but a decline followed in the 1870s in Great Stanmore and in the 1860s in Little Stanmore. Both populations rose again, Great Stanmore especially in the last decade of the century following the opening of a railway station in Old Church Lane in 1890.

## WHERE THE PEOPLE LIVED

Following the footsteps of the 1851 census enumerators is at once illuminating – showing where the concentrations of population were in the two villages – and confusing, as some of the roads were named differently from now. There were 229 inhabited houses in Great Stanmore, another 22 uninhabited ones and ten being built. 48 of the houses had two households within them. The two enumerators were David Martin, master of an academy at 10 High Street and Edmund Bailey, a draper at number 21.

David Martin started at Stanmore Park Farm and moved along the north side of Church Street (now Church Road). Next door but one to the Crown was Grove House, a 'Private Scholastic Establishment'. According to the enumerator this was number one. Between numbers 3 and 4 Church Street lay Belvedere Place with four houses, inhabited by laundresses, labourers and charwomen. Tomlin's Alley with a similar class of inhabitants was between 8 and 9. There were several tradesmen in Church Street itself. Upon leaving number 14, he turned up the west side of the High Street (now Stanmore Hill). There were 51 houses up to the junction with Green Lane with three houses in Engine Yard between 44 and 45. Almswomen lived in Engine Yard, where the fire engine had been housed. Beyond number 51 lay ten houses called The Square. These were probably small

*133. Church Road early this century looking towards the foot of Stanmore Hill. The house on the right is Sion House built before 1888. Later it became the telephone exchange.*

*134. The population of Great and Little Stanmore parishes 1801-1901.*

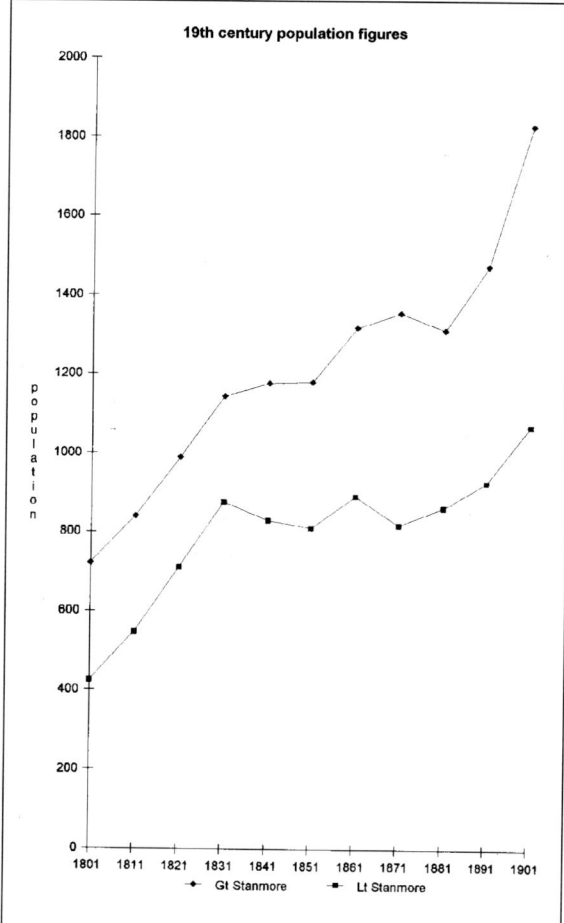

135. *The 18th-century building (since demolished) opposite the foot of Stanmore Hill is the original Queen's Head. By the time this photograph was taken about 1870, the pub had moved across the road.*

houses as they were lived in by farm labourers, paupers and errand boys. Pynnacles Place came next and then Mr Martin made his way along the houses opposite at the top of Green Lane, then carried on up Stanmore Hill past Aylwards and the brewery to the lodge of Bentley Priory, where his walk ended.

Edmund Bailey began at Marsh Farm and walked up Old Church Lane and along the south side of Church Street and along the High Road (now the Broadway), ending at Manor Farm (sometimes called Wards Farm and apparently the eastern end of the present Cottrell's Cottages). He crossed the road to two cottages at the bottom of Dennis Lane, then returned on the north side of the High Road. After Buckingham House where George Kirby, junior, a carpenter lived, Mr Bailey turned up the east side of the High Street (Stanmore Hill), then cut across to the common, south of Stanmore Hall. Having visited Warren House and the Grove, he returned to the High Street near the Vine Inn, then went around Little Common. He completed his walk down the High Street.

William Ham, a carpenter who lived in Watling Street, was the sole enumerator for Little Stanmore where there were fewer houses, 143 inhabited and 8 uninhabited. He began in Watling Street at Burnt Oak, went around Whitchurch Lane, Canons, the cottages opposite Stanmore Pound, Canons Park Lodges, the Lymes, Wood Lane and the turnpike road (Watling Street) to Elstree.

## EARNING A LIVING

The Stanmores were set in rural Middlesex and the vast majority of the land was farmed, so it is hardly surprising that the parishes were affected by the state of agriculture. On the other hand a large percentage of the population was earning a living from manufacture and shopkeeping by 1851, which must have given an urban character to the village centres. In the two parishes the largest number of employed people, 195, were in domestic service because of the spread of gentry houses in the neighbourhood described in earlier chapters. 105 were engaged in some form of manufacturing and seventy in dealing and shopkeeping. Another 56 were in some form of the building trade and only 74 were working in agriculture. The spread of occupations in the middle of the century is shown in the graph on the following page.

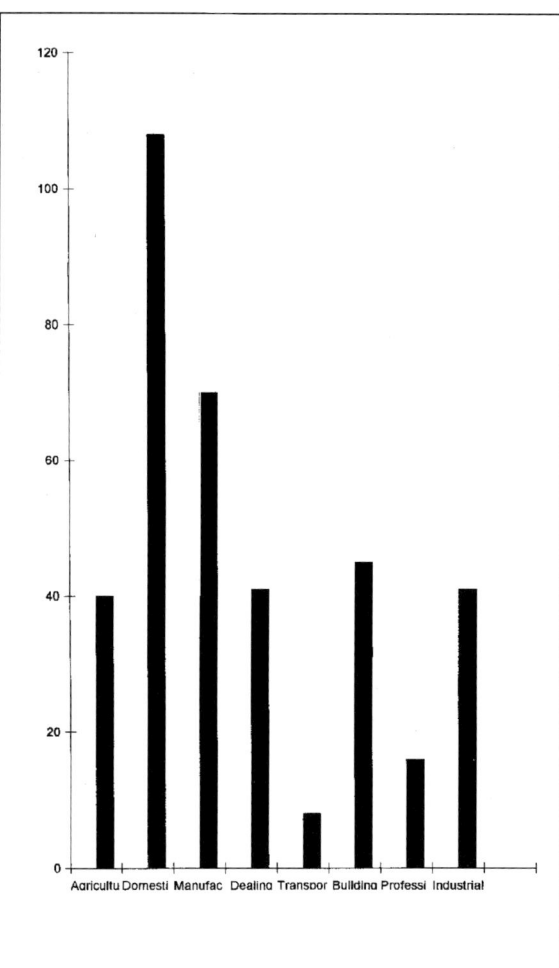

*136. Occupations in Great Stanmore in 1851.*

## FARMING

The gradual decline in agriculture in the two parts of Stanmore is depicted in the table at the foot of this page. The figures are taken from the Ministry of Agriculture's returns for the years 1867-1917.[1]

The greater number of people farming land in the later periods is due to thirty smallholdings of less than twenty acres, created by splitting off from bigger farms. More farmland disappeared in Great than in Little Stanmore because building started earlier in that parish.

The proximity of London with its horse powered transport needing hay for fuel, meant that less than 200 acres of land in the Stanmores were under the plough at the beginning of the nineteenth century and very lttle indeed by the end, when most of the fields were laid down to grass. Wheat and beans were the main arable crops in 1801, with a few acres of oats, potatoes and turnips. Root crops had replaced beans as the second largest crop by 1867 and wheat had gone out of production altogether by 1917, with potatoes, turnips and mangolds being principally grown on such arable as was left.

There were four main farms in Great Stanmore in the Victorian period, the Home Farm (sometimes called Park Farm) attached to Stanmore Park, Old Church Farm in Old Church Lane, Marsh Farm at the marsh and Manor Farm in the High Road. The 1851 census shows that Park Farm was only 74 acres in extent, but the farmer had a workforce of four. The house at Marsh Farm was occupied by the Perpetual Curate of Little Stanmore and the land appears to have been farmed with Old Church Farm at the time. Down Old Church Lane lived Henry Lewin, a farmer employing seven labourers, presumably working the lands of both farms together. Along the High Road, apparently on the corner of Marsh Lane, was Vere Woodman

| PLACE | YEAR | ACREAGE FARMLAND | FARMERS/SMALL HOLDERS |
|---|---|---|---|
| GREAT STANMORE | 1867 | 1333 | |
| | 1897 | 967 | 19 |
| | 1917 | 847 | 16 |
| LITTLE STANMORE | 1867 | 1363 | 10 |
| | 1897 | 1220 | 21 |
| | 1917 | 1183 | 18 |

137. *This picture, dated 1910, shows the old Queen's Head on the left and the new Queen's Head on the right. Beyond lies Sion House. Banks replaced the old Queen's Head in the 1920s. The buildings on the right have also been lost to Lloyd's Bank and office blocks.*

working Manor Farm with only one man. The position suggests that this farmhouse was actually the eastern end of the long, jettied building today known as Cottrell's Cottages and this is confirmed by a plan attached to a 1914 sales brochure,[2] at which time it was called Old Church Farm. The house in Old Church Lane seems to have lost its status and become an agricultural worker's cottage.

The Grove and Stanmore Hall had their own farms and there was Crab Tree Farm near the Grove, but only a labourer occupied it in 1851. In that year there were 21 agricultural labourers and 13 farm labourers living in Great Stanmore, some of whom may have been employed in neighbouring parishes. A cowman, horsekeeper and haybinder were the only other agricultural workers.

In the eighteenth century the 1st Duke of Chandos's farms in Little Stanmore were Grubs Farm, Old Farm and New Farm, amounting to over 200 acres. In 1851 there were five farmers working 880 acres between them. William Carter who had only 45 acres, lived with a relative, Thomas, who had 115 acres at Brockley Hill Farm. Thomas Henderson had 330 acres and employed twelve labourers. Since a farm bailiff lived in his house, this was probably the chief farm of the Canons estate. Francis Simpson employed nine men on 300 acres, while Charles Mead at Elstree Hill had 90 acres and three men.

There were 25 agricultural labourers, three farm; labourers and three farm servants in Little Stanmore. The distinction between the two types of labourer is hard to determine, but the farm servants were probably hired by the year at hiring fairs.

## DOMESTIC SERVICE

Great Stanmore had the larger number of house servants because of the proliferation of the middle class, but Little Stanmore had far more general servants, associated with the shops, inns and beerhouses along Watling Street. Butlers were to be found only at houses like The Warren, The Grove and Canons Park and footmen were thin on the ground, one being employed by the Perpetual Curate of Little Stanmore and another at the Manor House by Charles Otway Mayne. Lt Col. Hamilton Tovey Tennent had both a butler and footman at Pynnacles as well as a cook, kitchen maid, house maid and maid. Professional men like Francis King, the Veterinary Surgeon living at the former Fiddles at the corner of Dennis Lane, usually had two house servants, while a boot and shoemaker such as Benjamin Conquer in the High Street only had a maid of all work. William Adam, a West India merchant on Stanmore Hill at the house next to the brewery, was sufficiently well off to employ five house servants, while the brewer, James Wilshin, who employed 30 men, had just a cook and a housemaid.

*138. A view up Stanmore Hill*

## SHOPS AND SERVICES

Taken together the shopkeepers and tradesmen of the Stanmores provided comprehensive services for the inhabitants. Ten bakers, eight grocers, eleven butchers, four fishmongers and a cheesemonger provided ample choice of food. Sixteen dressmakers and eight tailors supplied clothes and there were nearly twenty boot and shoemakers and cordwainers making footwear. There were several milliners in Little Stanmore, umbrellas could be obtained from two makers, and drapers supplied materials. There was a watchmaker in Great Stanmore and, unusually for a country village, a historical engraver, George T. Doo and a bookseller, Alfred Greene who lived in the High Street and was also registrar. This unusually high number of shops, when compared with neighbouring villages may be due to the large number of gentlemen's residences all around.

There were plenty of bricklayers, sawyers, carpenters and plumbers in the village for new building work and about ten painter/glaziers to put the finishing touches to new houses. An ironmonger's shop was also useful.

There was a post office run by Priscilla Warrell, a letter-carrier in Little Stanmore and a postboy and postman in Great Stanmore. Their jobs were made easier by the fact that all the houses in the main roads were numbered.

Several drivers lived in the area. James Edward Benn of 24 High Street drove the mails and Elizabeth Castle of 7 Pynnacles Place gave her occupation as an omnibus driver! Perhaps that was her husband's job. There was a carrier and several carters, but six of them were lodging at the White Lion on Watling Street and were probably just passing through.

There were seven policemen to keep order, although there was as yet no police station. The one in Little Stanmore was built on the present site in Whitchurch Lane in 1865.

## DRINKING PLACES

The established inns, the Crown, the Abercorn Arms, the Vine and the Queen's Head, all flourished in Great Stanmore, along with the Green Man, a beer-house at the Marsh and another beer house in the High Street kept by Priscilla Wiggins. Watling Street had the Load of Hay, which was

139.  *Looking down Stanmore Hill, from near the junction with Green Lane.*

140.  *Nos. 83-85 Stanmore Hill, the post office in 1920.  Thomas George Berwick was postmaster.  John Seabrook at the Abercorn Arms was the first postmaster of Stanmore in 1828.*

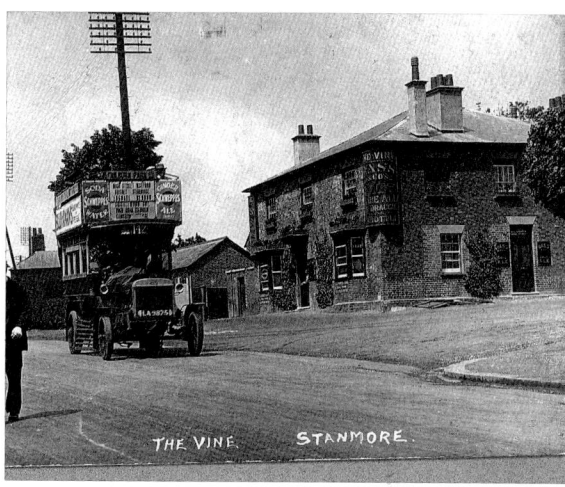

141. (below)  Little Stanmore north of Whitchurch Lane. Some of these buildings have been restored and are in better condition today than at the beginning of this century.

142. (above)  The Vine on the corner of Little Common.

143.  *Tramlines were being laid outside the White Lion when this photograph was taken in February 1904.*

144.  *Clutterbuck's Brewery on Stanmore Hill was taken over by Cannon Brewery in 1923.  H. Pattison & Co. carried on a turf maintenance and golf course equipment business in the buildings from 1926-28.  Charles Church Estates Ltd took over the property and the granary was demolished in 1988 and other buildings were converted into flats, known at first as Bentley Gate and latterly as Lancaster House.*

*145. Old Forge Close.*

*146. The brewer's house next door to the Brewery called The Rookery.*

a beer shop, and four inns, the White Hart, the White Lion, the Crane (Chandos Arms) and the Masons' Arms. There was also a beer shop in Brockley Hill and William Poulter had a small brewery near the Crane.

A much larger brewery was to be found on Stanmore Hill, belonging to the Clutterbuck family. Their brewhouse with its attractive cupola still stands with two eighteenth-century houses in the yard. Clutterbuck's Brewery, with a workforce of thirty, was the largest single employer in Stanmore in 1851. James Wilshin living in the adjacent house and another member of the Wilshin family, Henry, living nearby at Stanmore Villa were the brewers (presumably managers). Thomas Clutterbuck appears in the Great Stanmore court rolls in 1749, being admitted to the brewery and later in 1798 to the Vine, the Crown and other lands and cottages, formerly in the occupation of Daniel Rogers.

## THE PROFESSIONS

Little Stanmore had eight teachers. John Earle was the principal of Edgware House Commercial School where he had two teachers and forty students in Watling Street near the White Lion. Simon Van Vugt was the master of the Free School which had been established by Sir Lancelot Lake in 1656 and Ann Spicer who was 75, was the mistress of the Day School (this may have been the National School said to have been in existence by 1823). She had a young assistant, Susan Dandy whose father was a general labourer, suggesting that she was a pupil teacher. William Rowland was another teacher at an educational establishment next to the White Hart.

Great Stanmore had five teachers. George Rumsey ran a 'Private Scholastic Establishment'

at Grove House, Church Street, but he only had four resident pupils. At 10 High Street, David Martin described himself as Master of the Academy, which suggests another private school. Lydia Pepler was mistress of the High Street Infant School which was situated in Stanmore Hill below the Abercorn Arms and had been founded by Miss Catherine Elizabeth Martin of Woodlands in 1845. Robert Roy and his wife, schoolmaster and schoolmistress lived at Dalton House between the Manor House and the Rectory. Possibly they ran the Great Stanmore National School of which there is otherwise no mention, but which is supposed to have been in existence in 1833.

The one barrister, Shiston Johnson, lived at Montagues with his young family and staff. He described himself on the census form as 'barrister, landed proprietor and auditor of the Lincoln and Rutlandshire District'.

The two general practitioners lived in the High Street on either side of the historical engraver. William Rogers had a son also called William, who was a surgeon, and Arthur Noverre had a surgeon's assistant in his household. William Rogers was living in the former workhouse. There were five or six nurses, but mainly employed in private households. Susannah Joel was presumably a monthly nurse. She was resident at Thomas Pickett's house in Watling Street. He was a groom and his wife had just given birth.

## THE GENTRY

As so often happened on the night of the census, many of the larger houses were occupied only by servants or caretakers, their owners presumably being at their town houses or visiting elsewhere.

147.  *Children from cottages near the Duck in Pond, playing near Belmont in 1910. The photographer provided the smocks and sunbonnets.*

# Passing the time

Inhabitants of rural communities usually found their entertainment in public houses and the working-class people of the Stanmores were no exception. But perhaps because of the prevalence of superior houses, the neighbourhood also boasted at one time an Assembly Room. John Snoxell had the Queen's Head and the Assembly Room in the 1750s and the two were probably associated to begin with. The Room seems to have functioned only in the eighteenth century and had been converted into six cottages by the time Edward Ironmonger Snoxell inherited it in 1810.[1] It is a pity that no programme relating to the entertainments put on there has survived. They probably included private balls such as the one described in Jane Austen's *Emma*.

John Snoxell had married Elizabeth Ironmonger whose family had kept the Queen's Head earlier in the eighteenth century: their monuments lie against the east and north walls of the ruined red brick church. Later the Queen's Head moved from its original position opposite the foot of Stanmore Hill to the western corner of Church Road and the hill. Robert Hollond of Stanmore Hall owned it and let it to Thomas Clutterbuck, the brewer.[2]

## INSTITUTES

Families like the Hollonds and the Bernays took their leading position in Stanmore society to heart and in paternalistic fashion provided institutes and libraries for the populace. The Bernays Institute, built in 1870 by the rector to commemorate his son, stands in the middle of Stanmore. A Working Men's Club was in existence by the 1890s in a building alongside. Immediately after the First World War an army hut around the back of the Institute was utilised by the Bernays' Trustees to provide a recreational club for women, as part of the war memorial. Though the full title of this club was 'the hut for the wives of working men and ladies' maids', it was always known as 'the hut'. Educational activities, sports and entertainment were provided. As the number of ladies' maids declined in later years the hall was neglected and practically derelict by 1965, the year when the local branch of the National Council of Women was formed. This needed a meeting place in order to expand and the Bernays' Trustees agreed to let them have the hut, provided that they maintained it. The NCW re-roofed, re-floored and repainted it and gave it a new name, 'Glebe Hall'. The land was formerly part of the rector's glebe. The NCW let it out as well as holding their own meetings and other activities there. 550 functions took place in 1997, suggesting that it still plays

148. *The Bernays Institute, given to the people of Stanmore by the Revd Leopold Bernays in memory of his son, Ernest, who drowned while on holiday in Switzerland.*

**A Library for Stanmore.**—A library was opened at the Institute, Stanmore, on Saturday last, when, under new auspices, the old collection of books with new ones promises to supply a long felt want in Stanmore. Mrs Pritchard and Mrs Devitt were the chief movers in the undertaking, the former acting as librarian. The library consists now of over 700 volumes, and is worked in connection with Mudies. Most of the tradesmen have subscribed, and are supporting the institution. The rules regarding subscriptions are—subscribers to pay 2s 6d a year, or 4d a month for two volumes of the old collection or one of the new, and non-subscribers 1d a vol, Mudies books 2d a vol. Also non-subscribers may use the library by the payment of 5s a year. The library is to be opened from 12 to 1 every Saturday for the changing of books. Other times probably will be arranged as the institution increases.

149. *The new library, advertised in the local paper in 1899.*

an important role in Stanmore's social life.[3] The Institute and the Working Men's Club (which has been rebuilt more than once) also flourish. All three buildings remain in the ownership of the Bernays' Trustees.

At Whitchurch Lane the former National School was merged with the old Lake Charity (*see p103*) and the building was made available for public use. It housed a Working Men's Club for Little Stanmore and other activities and was always known as the Institute. After it was swept away by a road-widening scheme in 1930, a new Whitchurch Institute was built on the corner of Buckingham Road and Chandos Crescent.

## LIBRARIES

When the Stanmore Hall estate was put up for sale in 1888, Lot 8 was described as a baker's shop in the occupation of Mr Benn, 'adjoining premises known as Stanmore Library and Reading Room … at present devoted by the vendor [Mr Hollond] to the purpose of the library and reading room and residential apartments for the manager'. The two premises were on the north side of Elm House (now no. 17 Stanmore Hill)  A new library was opened at the Bernays' Institute in 1899.

## SPORT

Football and cricket were popular pastimes. Stanmore Cricket Cub was granted the cricket ground out of the manorial waste by the Lord of the Manor in 1853. William Smith Tootell received the ground from the Marquess of Abercorn on behalf of trustees and it has been in use ever since.

150. *A picture taken outside the Whitchurch Institute on election day 1906, when the Hon. W.H. Peel, the local Conservative candidate, visited the polling stations. He was narrowly defeated by the Liberal, James Gibb.*

*151.  A cricket match on Stanmore Common in 1853, the year the Stanmore CC was formed.*

*152.  Stanmore Athletic Football Club 1912-13.*

*153.  Members of Stanmore Cricket Club in 1890.*

*154. A view of the gasometers at Stanmore Marsh about 1930.*

# Local Essentials

## A GAS SERVICE

Gas was the earliest public utility to be provided for the people of Stanmore. John Chapman, a Harrow ironmonger, had started a gas works at Harrow and wished to extend the service to Stanmore in 1858. The Stanmore Gas Company was founded with the Revd L.J. Bernays as chairman and land was provided for gasometers at Stanmore Marsh. Their successors are there still. On the day when the villages of Great and Little Stanmore, Edgware and Bushey Heath were lighted with gas for the first time, a celebratory dinner was held at the Abercorn Arms, presided over by Mr Bernays. The outside of the pub was illuminated by two gas-lit stars placed against the wall and there was a fine pyrotechnical display. The company became the Harrow and Stanmore Gas in 1894; it was taken over by the Brentford Gas Company in 1924 and merged with the Gas, Light and Coke Company in 1926. The Company provided street lighting in 1929.

## ELECTRICITY

Electricity was supplied from 1906 by the Northwood Electric Light and Power Company.

## CLEANER WATER

There had always been water available in Great Stanmore from the many ponds on the common and in the fields. It was piped down from a great pond on the common to the Manor House as early as 1640 and later a pond was dug on the north side of the Broadway to collect surface water. In the nineteenth century piped water from the Spring Pond at Little Common supplemented the surface water and pumps stood beside both ponds. The one at the Spring Pond is still in situ, but neither pond nor pump survive at the Broadway. Other pumps and wells for use by subscribers, and in some cases, paupers, are mentioned in the court rolls. The Round Pump and well by Great Stanmore church were apparently in some kind of housing, which was often locked to prevent the supply being exhausted. The only public pump available to the people of Little Stanmore, was near the churchyard of St Margaret's, Edgware.

These sources of supply were not always satisfactory as becomes clear from a report[1] made in 1873 when the Colne Valley Water Company proposed laying pipes in the district. The water in the field ponds was tainted with manure; that in the large ponds was often too dirty even to wash floors; while the pond in the Broadway was frequently choked with weeds, filthy with animal and vegetable life and sometimes had drowned

155.  *The Spring Pond at Little Common and the pump.*

156. *The pond on the north side of the Broadway which collected surface water and was supplemented by water piped down from the Spring Pond. Note Cottrell's Cottages in the middle distance.*

157. *This water fountain at the junction of Green Lane and Stanmore Hill was given by Charles Keyser's sister, Agnes. She lived with him at Warren House. The bowl is now on the corner of Old Church Lane, by the churchyard.*

158.  *The constancy of the local water supply was of great importance to the local fire brigade.  This picture shows the Edgware firemen who dealt with fires in Stanmore.  The fire station was at the back of the Chandos Arms.*

animals floating in it. There were such queues for the pump by Edgware Church that one enterprising lady took buckets of water around the parish in a donkey cart, selling them for a penny a pail.

Several local gentlemen were among the founders of the Colne Valley Water Company in 1873, which could supply pure water from its gathering grounds in the Chilterns. Charles Keyser of Warren House was the first chairman of the company and John Robert Hollond of Stanmore, the second. The Colne Valley supply was thankfully accepted.

Both parishes had Nuisance Removal Committees in the 1850s and there were sewers, albeit open ones in the 1860s. These were enclosed first in earthenware and later in iron pipes and there was a main sewer running down Old Church Lane by 1871.[2] Edgware and Little Stanmore Sewage Farm was opened in Kingsbury in 1896 for surrounding parishes. This served until the Middlesex Sewerage Scheme came into being in 1933 and the Stanmores sewage was dealt with at the Mogden Sewerage Works near Isleworth. Perhaps because of the smallness of the population relatively little is heard of serious outbreaks of disease. When 'low fever' was prevalent in Little Stanmore in 1858, the Nuisance Committee confessed itself mystified as to the cause.

## HOSPITALS
### Stanmore Cottage Hospital
Emily and Katherine Wickens, who lived at the Pynnacles, paid for the building of a cottage hospital in Old Church Lane, near the new Stanmore Station, in 1890-1. John F. Curwen's design to provide three wards, for men, women and children, was only partially built. Instead, there was a female ward with four beds and a cot and a three-bedded male ward. The doctor's house in Green Lane (Clodiagh), was not always used as such. The hospital was transformed into an old people's home when the National Health Service was started in 1948 and served that purpose until 1980. For about four years, 1981-1985, it was run by the Jewish Society for the Mentally Handicapped. It continued to be a home for mentally-handicapped adults, under the auspices of the Ravenswood Foundation, until 1997 when it closed down.

### Isolation Hospital
Scarlet fever and diphtheria were prevalent and dangerous diseases in Victorian and Edwardian times and it was a great step forward when an Isolation Hospital was opened in Honeypot Lane in 1902. It became a residential nursery in 1948.

## Royal National Orthopaedic Hospital

The most famous hospital in Stanmore is the Royal National Orthopaedic, which opened its country branch at the top of Brockley Hill in 1920, taking over existing buildings. Miss Mary Wardell owned a house called Sulloniacae near the corner of Wood Lane and Brockley Hill, which she converted into a convalescent home for children suffering from infectious diseases in 1882. The salubrious air was good for them. During the First World War it was used as a Military Hospital and afterwards it was bought by the Shaftesbury Society and then by the Royal National Orthopaedic. Miss Wardell had by then died, but had set up a trust requiring that any future use should incorporate an element of convalescence. As the buildings were to be used as a country outpost of the main hospital these criteria were fulfilled. The hospital opened in 1922 and quickly purchased more land along Wood Lane and down the north side of Brockley Hill, eventually owning 115 acres, including Mr Sharpe's Sulloniacae obelisk. Miss Wardell's hospital was extended and new wards were built.

A training college and workshops on the site replaced the Wrights Lane Home for Crippled

*160. The Cottage Hospital was built in Old Church Lane in 1891, close to the station.*

Boys, Kensington, in 1937. These were put to a different use in 1948, part of the workshops being leased to the Institute of Orthopaedics. There have been many changes in more recent years, with much emphasis on mobility and independence. A lot of building is going on in the grounds in 1998.

*159. The Royal National Orthopaedic Hospital opened a country outpost at Brockley Hill in 1922.*

# The Local Schools

As is evident from the histories of houses like Bentley Priory, Stanmore Park, Hill House and The Cottage below Stanmore Hall, recounted in earlier chapters, and from the Victorian census returns, there were usually private schools situated in Stanmore from the eighteenth century onwards. What of the village children? Was there any provision for them?

Sir Lancelot Lake, who died in 1680, built a schoolhouse with a market hall underneath in Little Stanmore and arranged for trustees to administer a piece of land at Stanmore marsh, so as to pay a schoolmaster £15 a year. After Lake's death the schoolhouse also passed to the trustees, and the money arising from this endowment continued to help fund education in Little Stanmore until the present century. In 1604 Sir Lancelot's

*162. Edgware House, seen here in 1967, housed a private commercial school in the mid-19th century. John Earle was the principal and he had 40 students in 1851, but only 21 ten years later.*

*161. Stanmore Infants' School built in Stanmore Hill in 1845 at the expense of the benevolent Miss Martin of Woodlands.*

father, Sir Thomas Lake, had been granted the right to hold a weekly market and two fairs a year. The building of the market hall suggests that the markets were held there in the seventeenth century, but they must have died out by 1749, when the schoolmaster of the day was given permission to convert part of it to his own use. The income from the rented land rose from time to time, reaching £60 by 1823, but only £30 was paid to the schoolmaster, and £10 went to the organist. The school was free to pupils and occasionally the Vestry ordered that books should be bought for their use. From about 1820 there was a National School as well in Little Stanmore but the free school continued, usually with about thirty pupils, and Simon von Vught was the master in 1851. In 1855 a new National School opened in Whitchurch Lane, replacing the free school, but in its turn it was amalgamated with Edgware Board School in 1896.

The buildings were then used as a Sunday School and as an Institute (see previous chapter) and £15 a year from Lake's endowment was to be granted to local children, some of whom might be at institutes of higher education. In 1905 this became known as Sir Lancelot Lake's Educational Foundation.

## Great Stanmore

A National School opened in Great Stanmore in 1826, but its site is not known. There were sixty pupils, twenty boys and forty girls in 1833. There was also an Infants' School in that year. Miss Catherine Martin of Woodlands in Stanmore Hill gave land on the opposite side of the hill as a site for a new Infants' School which opened in 1845. Here there was room for 100 children in a single room, although there were never so many attending, and a mistress's house adjoining. The National School moved to a new site to the south of the Infants' School in 1861 and had three classrooms and a teacher's house. Both schools were enlarged in the 1880s, perhaps reflecting the growing number of cottages in Stanmore and both were ordered to have improvements to bring them up to standard in 1904. In 1960 a new school called St John's was built in Green Lane and the juniors moved from the National School building into it. The infants moved out of their old school into the National School at the same time and in 1964 followed the juniors to St John's. Although built by the Middlesex County Council, the new school was managed by the London Diocesan Board of Education. It is now St John's Church of England School.

163. *The new National School erected south of the Infants' School and opened in 1861.*

## Suburban Schools

Camrose Primary School opened in Litle Stanmore in 1931 and Stag Lane School in 1935 in temporary huts in Collier Drive – new buildings were ready in 1937. Stanburn School also began in temporary accommodation in 1936 and moved to a new building in Abercorn Road two years later. These took care of the children from the new suburban housing spreading across the southern part of the area in the 1930s. Aylward School in Pangbourne Drive was built in 1952. A nursery for forty children started in a prefabricated bungalow on a bomb site in Buckingham Road in 1942, became the Buckingham Nursery School in 1946. Secondary education was provided by Camrose Secondary School, opened in 1932, Chandos Secondary School (1939) and Downer Grammar School (1952).

Education was reorganised into First Schools, Middle Schools and High Schools in the Borough of Harrow in 1974. Camrose Primary became Little Stanmore First and Middle School, Downer and Camrose joined to become Canons High School and Chandos Secondary was renamed Park High School. Stag Lane, Stanburn and Aylward primaries became First and Middle Schools, but retained their old names. Two new schools have been founded recently – Whitchurch First School in 1992 and Whitchurch Middle School in 1996. The first tertiary college to be built in the Borough of Harrow opened in Old Church Lane in 1969 as Elm Park College. It has since been renamed Stanmore Junior College. Nursery education is now available at several of the First Schools.

The North London Collegiate School was founded by the redoubtable pioneer of women's education, Frances Mary Buss. It opened in a house in Camden Town in 1850 to cater principally for the daughters of professionals and tradesmen,

*164. The main hall of the North London Collegiate School, one of the additions made to Canons since 1929.*

who often had little formal education at all. The school flourished and eventually moved to Camden Road where a new school was specially built. However, the school again became overcrowded and in 1929 bought Canons and some of its grounds to which pupils came on a regular basis from Camden Town. This shuttling of pupils continued until April 1940, when the whole school finally moved to Canons – fortuitously as it turned out, for their building in Camden Town received a direct hit in the bombing of the following year.

# The Leafy Suburb

## FREDERICK GORDON

Frederick Gordon (1835-1904), more than any other man, is responsible for the modern layout of the northern part of Great Stanmore. He purchased the Bentley Priory estate from John Kelk in 1881, (see p87), Stanmore Park in 1887, the Manor House and grounds in 1890, and Lord Halsbury's house, Woodlands, on Stanmore Hill in 1899, making himself master of 775 acres, just over half the parish. When Bentley Priory was advertised for sale in 1880, the brochure advised that there was a possibility of building on 200 acres. Mr Gordon in fact ran Bentley Priory as a hotel for a few years (1885-1890/1), but it was never very successful and he may always have had it in mind to develop the land. During the hotel period the Gordon family lived in a new house, Glenthorn (demolished since 1945), built in the grounds. It was embellished with the Gordon crest, a flexed bow and arrow.

## STANMORE STATION

Gordon was the main mover in getting a branch line built from the London & North-Western Railway station at Wealdstone to Stanmore. He held the controlling interest in the Harrow and Stanmore Railway Company formed in 1886 for that purpose and was chairman. Plans had been put forward for a line west of Belmont, with a station on the Uxbridge Road, but Gordon pushed for a route along the eastern edge of Stanmore Park and a terminus in Old Church Lane. He bought Stanmore Park to make this possible. On the occasion of the grand opening of the station on 18 December 1890 Gordon entertained the great and the good of the neighbourhood and the railway company with a reception and lunch in the covered tennis court at Bentley Priory, accompanied by music. 500 workmen, who were being fed in the wood sheds at the same time, had Harrow Brass Band to help their digestive juices. By the time the line opened he had laid out a road, Gordon Avenue, across the grounds to the station. Any

*165.  An invitation to the grand opening of the new branch railway from Harrow to Stanmore, 18 December 1890.*

*168.  The ecclesiastical style station buildings in Old Church Lane. The station closed in September 1952. This building, bereft of its tower, still stands as a private house.*

*166.  Some of the navvies who built the branch line.*

*167.  The very attractive flower-bedecked station platform at Stanmore.*

thoughts of attracting more visitors to the hotel by offering a rail connection with Town, seem to have been superseded by ideas of encouraging Londoners to live in the country in brand new superior houses.

## THE GORDON FAMILY

Frederick Gordon and his family were using Bentley Priory as a private residence in 1891.  Gordon had been born at Ross-on-Wye in 1835, where his father had moved from London and was a house

decorator. Later Mr Gordon senior returned to the capital and became a manager of dining rooms. Frederick trained as a solicitor, then became a very successful proprietor of restaurants and hotels, the First Avenue, Holborn and the Hotel Metropole in Northumberland Avenue being two among many. The Gordon Hotel Co. Ltd, set up in 1890, owned hotels nationwide and on the continent. He became associated in business with John Blundell Maple who furnished the hotels and was involved in mining ventures in the Ashanti mine-fields. Gordon had the Midas touch, remaining extremely wealthy even though some individual projects were not financially successful. His first wife, who died in 1869, left him with a son and a daughter and he married again, producing eight more sons and one more daughter. Ten of the children ranging in age from 25 to three were with him at Bentley Priory on the night of the 1891 census.

When planning the development of his broad estates he set the tone by not allowing trains to run into Stanmore on Sundays for fear of vulgar trippers destroying the peaceful ambience and the station itself was of ecclesiastical design. South of the building plots on Gordon Avenue, golf links were laid out and the Stanmore Golf Club opened in 1893, another bait for those aspiring to country life.

When Gordon died in 1904 at Cannes, whither he had repaired for the sake of his health to his own Hotel Metropole, the Stanmore estates were left in trust for his children. The whole was put up for auction in 1909 in 70 lots. However, they were bought in and the Stanmore Estate Company stayed in being until 1953, holding the freehold of most of the property.

## DEVELOPMENTS ON THE GORDON LANDS

The plans and sale details in the 1909 sale brochure show that most of the development up to that point had been along the roads around the station, Gordon Avenue and Old Church Lane. Some pairs of cottages in Old Church Lane called Stuart, Keith and Cameron, Hamilton and Vivian, Malcolm and Leslie Cottages were named after his children. They were three-bedroomed semi-detached pairs backing onto the Park Nursery and let on monthly tenancies and probably intended for the type of families that would provide gardeners and

*169.  The LMS Stanier class 2P 0-4-4T No. 6408 with the branch auto train returning to Harrow on 26 May 1934.*

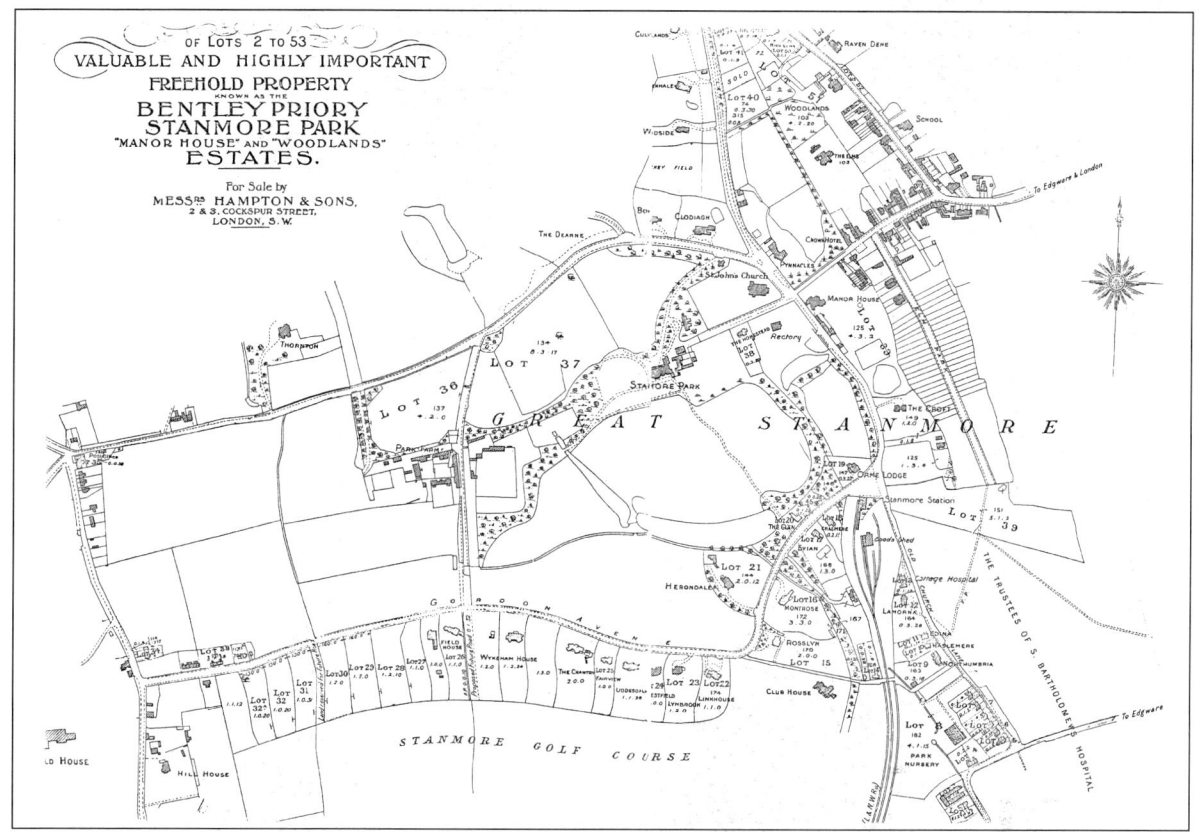

*170. Part of the Bentley Priory estate in 1909, showing some development.*

charladies for the 'high class' residences being built nearby. A slightly unusual erection was a 'substantial and attractively-built block of buildings known a Aberdeen Cottages', actually a block of eight self-contained flats, each equipped with gas, water and electric bells.

Houses called Tanglewood, Glenthorn (where the Gordon family had lived) and The Holt in Common Road west of the deer park and Benhale, Woodside, Bowls and Clodiagh on Green Lane and the corner of the Uxbridge Road, were the only developments in Bentley Priory's own grounds. One of the plots in Old Church Lane was occupied by the Cottage Hospital and Clodiagh was the doctor's house. High Elms and The Garth had filled in some of the garden frontage of Woodlands in Stanmore Hill. Other plots were still vacant.

The Manor House grounds had been divided into two and The Croft built at the southern end. The whole was purchased in 1930 by Samuel Wallrock who demolished the Manor House and transformed The Croft into the New Manor House

as described on p25. When he became bankrupt in 1933 the church took over the decorative outbuildings (partially used as a ballroom) for a church hall and other parts became the verger's residence. The northern part of the grounds were opened to the public as Bernays Gardens in 1948.

The new suburban houses were mainly large and impressive with at least five main bedrooms and dressing rooms, as well as the usual complement of drawing, morning and dining rooms downstairs. Bowls and Woodside were both designed by Arnold Mitchell between 1893 and 1896 and show the influence of Norman Shaw. James B. Scott was the architect of Cheyne Cottage in Gordon Avenue, built about 1910. Its most unusual feature was a bell turret, from which the bell was rung to summon the residents from the golf course when callers arrived. Unfortunately many of the interesting late Victorian and Edwardian houses in fairly large gardens tempted developers and infillers from the 1960s onwards and have largely disappeared, often remembered only in the names of the closes of smaller houses

"BOWLS," GREAT STANMORE.   ARNOLD MITCHELL, ARCHITECT.

*171.  Arnold Mitchell designed this house, Bowls, near the corner of Uxbridge Road and Green Lane in 1896.  It was demolished in 1962 to make way for Bowls Close.*

*172.  This view along Gordon Avenue shows Cheyne Cottage on the left.  The bell in the cupola called the residents from the adjoining golf course when visitors arrived.*

which replaced them.  Examples are Bowls Close and Woodside Close.

By 1939 inroads had been made north into Bentley Priory grounds from Uxbridge Road.  The former lodge, much extended, still stands at the corner of Old Lodge Way and Uxbridge Road.  Other roads like Priory Close have appeared on the Common side of Bentley Priory.

When the house at Bentley Priory ceased to be a girls' boarding school in 1925, it was purchased for the RAF and the ground south of the house, including Heriots Wood (the former Long Hedge) was purchased by Harrow Urban District Council in 1936 to be part of the green belt.  It is now Bentley Priory Open Space and administered by the Borough of Harrow.

## CANONS PARK

As related on p25, the trustees of Dr Begg's widow put the Canons estate up for auction in 1887.  Morris Jenks bought it only to sell it on to the Canons Park Estate Company in 1896.  In 1887 the land stretched north from Whitchurch Lane across London Road to the bottom of Cloisters Wood.  The woodland, which had been part of the Chandos estate in the eighteenth century, belonged in 1887 to Charles Keyser of the Warren House.  Marsh Lane and Dennis Lane formed the western bound-

173. *Oak Lodge or Villa on the corner of Dennis Lane and London Road, built about 1850. The photograph is dated 1891.*

ary of the estate and Edgware High Street/Stone Grove the eastern boundary as far north as London Road. Fields between Pear Wood and Brockley Hill were separately owned.

Apart from the lodges, two of which had four and six bedrooms and servants' accommodation, there were four 'superior detached residences' at the corner of Dennis Lane and London Road and Stone Grove Cottage and Stone Grove House on either side of Stone Grove Lodge. The houses at the corner of Dennis Lane, Oak Villa, Vine Cottage, Townsend Villa and one unnamed, had been leased to John Wilson from 1849 and may have been built about that time. Stone Grove House with its seven bedrooms and a boudoir was let to C.E.O. Pritchard Esq and described as 'old fashioned', which would certainly mean nothing later than the eighteenth century. Apart from this there were Marsh Farm House let to William Hale and four cottages in Marsh Lane. Three near the corner of London Road were described as timbered and thatched. About half an acre in Whitchurch Lane, occupied by Mr Ingold as a timber yard was suitable for the erection of cottages.

The Canons Park Estate Company produced plans for development, but Arthur Du Cros bought the whole estate, retaining the mansion, but selling part of the land in 1905. Whitchurch Gardens were being built on it in 1911. After Sir Arthur (as he became) formed a trust in 1920 and the mansion and remaining grounds were again available for sale, the real development of Little Stanmore began. George Cross and Canons Ltd bought the building land and the North London Collegiate School took the mansion and ten acres, acquiring more playing fields in 1936. Harrow UDC laid out the old walled garden as the George V Memorial Garden in 1936 and the other land bought by the council survives as a public park, complete with the remnant of the old north/south avenue of trees. Other survivals from the Duke of Chandos's time are the lake in the north-eastern corner of the gardens and the basin in the middle of Canons Drive. The houses built by ADC Properties Ltd from 1928 onward were known as DC houses and survive fifty to sixty years later as desirable residences.

## THE FARMLANDS TO THE SOUTH

The governors of St Bartholomew's Hospital started negotiating with the trustees of the Marquess of Abercorn to buy Old Church Farm, Marsh Farm and Kenton Lane Farm, the latter mainly lying in Harrow Weald, in 1853. The final agreement was reached in September 1856.[1] Marsh Farm House and ten acres were sold by the Hospital to Dr Begg and was subsequently known as Canons Park Farm. Old Church Farm House (the eastern end of Cottrell's Cottages)[2] and 3½ acres were offered for sale by St Bartholomew's in 1914, as 'suitable for the erection of a public institution or modern shops and the remainder...is well adapted for detached and semi-detached residences, similar to those recently erected opposite'. The main sales of the Hospital's farmland in Stanmore began in 1926, the largest single sale being to John Laing & Co. in 1934.

Council houses were provided in Wolverton Road and on the glebe land behind the Bernays' Institute and on the Berridge and Chandos estates in Little Stanmore.

*175. A shuttle service between Stanmore and Wembley Park was run at first. This Metropolitan Railway Driving Motor Coach No. 69 is setting off from Stanmore on 5 August 1934.*

*174. A modern style house erected on Kerry Avenue to the designs of Gerald Ducoste.*

## MODERN TRANSPORT

The spread of housing in the south was greatly encouraged by the opening of Belmont Station in 1932 on the L&NWR line and by the building of the Metropolitan Line extension from Wembley Park through Kingsbury to a terminus at Little Stanmore just south of the London Road in the same year. Honeypot Lane was improved about the same time. Canons Park Station opened in 1935 where a shopping parade was built. The Metropolitan Line extension became the Bakerloo Line in 1939 and subsequently the Jubilee Line. The earliest station in the area at Edgware in 1867 on the Great Northern Branch Line did not lead to much development because Mrs Begg seems to have had no wish to cut up Canons. The Edgware underground station of 1924 may, however, have influenced George Cross to start building.

Trams of the Metropolitan Electric Tramways Company and buses of London General Omnibus Company ran to Little Stanmore from 1907. The trams stopped at the corner of London Road, but some buses continued to Watford. By 1934 buses served Great Stanmore and Elstree.

The L&NWR had taken over the running of the branch line to Stanmore soon after its opening and continued until the nationalisation of the railways and the formation of British Rail in 1948. Thirty-six trains were running each way on weekdays in 1950 when the station was renamed Stanmore Village Station to avoid confusion with the London Transport Stanmore Station. By that time the line was said to be losing £4000 a week and the station was closed down in 1952 when the section from Belmont was no longer used. The branch line itself closed in 1964 and the station was converted to a private house. September Way covers the station and goods yard area.

## THE ROYAL AIR FORCE

The Royal Air Force presence at Bentley Priory since 1926 and Stanmore Park since 1938 has had the physical effect of maintaining some open ground in Stanmore, but on the other hand married quarters crept across the landscape, especially the roads off Old Church Lane and The Chase.

From 1926 Bentley Priory was the Head Quarters of Inland Area, responsible for training in the ADGB organisation (Air Defence of Great Britain). Between 1934-39 the number of Home Defence Squadrons was scheduled to be increased from 42 to 107. Fighter Command Head Quarters opened

*176. The Filter Room at Bentley Priory during the Second World War.*

at Bentley Priory on 14 July 1936 under the command of Air Chief Marshal Hugh Dowding. The Observer Corps which had been formally established in 1925 moved to Bentley Priory in 1936 as well to be part of Fighter Command. In the run up to the war an underground operations block was built which was occupied in 1940. Barrage balloon defences around London also had to be improved and Stanmore Park was acquired by the RAF in 1938 to be Balloon Command Head Quarters. Air Vice-Marshal O.T. Boyd was in charge at Stanmore Park. Anti-Aircraft Command moved into Frederick Gordon's house, Glenthorn, in 1939 and adopted the Gordon crest of flexed bow and arrow as its badge. During hostilities the underground Ops Room and Filter Room at Bentley Priory, were at the heart of the whole system, information being filtered from there around the country.

Bentley Priory survived the war remarkably well, with nothing worse than the shattering of window glass by the blast of a V2 rocket, but was severely damaged by fire in 1947 and had to be restored. It became the headquarters of No 11 (F) Group and of Strike Command Administration in 1968. By 1974 the house was considerably the worse for wear because of dry rot and practically condemned by the Department of the Environment. The whole place was devastated by fire in 1979. Eventually it was decided to restore the building and much research was undertaken, especially into any remaining parts of the Soane structure. The work was completed in 1991.

Samuel Wallrock's New Manor House was taken over by the RAF in 1940 and is still in 1998 the Air Commodore's house. Officers' houses were built in the grounds and a section between the MOD houses and Bernays Gardens has been filled with Tudor Well Close. The well at the corner was one of the many antique features placed in the grounds of the Manor House by Samuel Wallrock.

Bentley Priory with its beautiful old building at its heart, is the Head Quarters for Number 11 Corps, the Royal Observer Corps and is the System Development Centre for the United Kingdom.[3] Stanmore Park, although still MOD property, no longer operates as a base. Operational use ceased in April 1997 and in January 1998 a residential development with a school was under discussion. The loss of Stanmore Park itself, so abruptly demolished in 1938 can only continue to be a cause for regret. The restoration of Bentley Priory by the RAF in 1990-1 is, however, a bonus.

177.  Glenthorn was built in the grounds of Bentley Priory for Frederick Gordon and his family. It became the HQ of Anti-Aircraft Command during the war.

178.  Clement Attlee and his wife lived at Heywood in London Road until moving to Downing Street as prime minister in 1945. Later the house became a nursing home and was demolished in 1978. Flats now occupy the site.

# Modern Times

Nowadays, the division between Great and Little Stanmore is almost forgotten except by long standing inhabitants, one of whom having lived on the Glebe estate for some sixty years, told the author, with a twinkle in his eye, that he is still looked upon as a foreigner, because he was born in Little Stanmore, fully a mile distant from his present home. The two churches, St John's and St Lawrence's retain their separate parishes for ecclesiastical purposes, and as the second millennium of Christianity approaches, both are well cared for by flourishing congregations, although a smaller proportion of the population now attends church than when they were founded fairly early in the first millennium.

Suburban Stanmore has a population of about 30,000 in the late 1990s, giving a lower density than other parts of the Borough of Harrow. Much of the northern area remains open land, as Stanmore Common, part of Bentley Priory Open Space, Cloisters and Pear Woods and the grounds of the Royal National Orthopaedic Hospital. Further south there are Stanmore Golf Club, Canons Park and several sports grounds. Stanmore has been fortunate in retaining so much greenery, well maintained and much of it open to the public. The fate of the old rural buildings has been less happy.

Anyone who stands on the corner of Whitchurch Lane today and compares the urban traffic-ridden wasteland with the scene depicted in the photograph on page 6, can only be sickened at the thought of the attractive timber-framed buildings that were torn down in the early and middle years of this century and wonder who has benefited by the destruction.

The centre of Stanmore has only Cottrell's Cottages and a small timber-framed house with an eighteenth-century front, crammed between much taller office blocks, left, despite the unceasing efforts of the Stanmore & Harrow Historical Society. Cottages and old pubs like The Fountain have given way to offices with shops beneath and the new Automobile Association building overshadows the Bernays Institute. A supermarket has come and gone and a new one is in contemplation to fill the gap left by the old AA building. Will there also be a cinema? Stanmore is one of the few suburbs bypassed by Oscar Deutch. The small shops tend here, as in other London suburbs in the 1990s, to sell little more than tobacco, newspapers and prepared food, so residents shop in Edgware. This is a marked social change, because for many years after the Second World War, practically all household needs were catered for on the spot, as was apparently the case back in the 1850s. The Abercorn Arms, still in its original building, and the old houses on Little Common and Stanmore Hill provide a pleasant feeling of continuity with the elegant past.

*179. Modern Stanmore – a timber-framed house with an eighteenth-century facade almost overwhelmed by commercial buildings in Church Road.*

# Sources

**Early Times**
[1]   Walter W. Druett, *The Stanmores and Harrow Weald through the ages* 13 (1938).
[2]   Robert Ellis, 'Excavations in Grim's Dyke, Harrow' *Transactions of the London & Middlesex Archaeological Society* 33, 173-176 (1982).
[3]   Stephen A. Castle, 'Excavations in Pear Wood, Brockley Hill, Stanmore' *Transactions of the London & Middlesex Archaeological Society* 26, 267-277 (1975).
[4]   David Bowsher 'An evaluation of the Roman road at Brockley Hill, Middlesex' *Transactions of the London & Middlesex Archaeological Society* 46, 45-57 (1995).
[5]   David Bowsher *ibid.*
[6]   *Cart. Sax,* ed Birch, I, 373
[7]   David Sullivan, *The Westminster Corridor,* 110 and 167 (1994).

**The Manors of Stanmore**
[1]   Druett, *op. cit.,* Chapter V written by Trelawney Roberts.
[2]   *Ibid,* Chapters VI & VII.
[3]   The full story can be pursued in Druett *op. cit;* Percy Davenport *Old Stanmore;* and the *Victoria County History, Middlesex,* Vol. V.
[4]   Druett *op. cit.,* Chapters VI & VII
[5]   *VCH Middlesex,* Vol. V, 98.
[6]   *Ibid,* 98.
[7]   Denoon and Roberts 'An extent of Edgware with Kingsbury' *Transactions of the London & Middlesex Archaeological Society* XVIII, 160 (1933).
[8]   E.A. Webb, *Records of St Bartholomew's, Smithfield,* 1, 166.
[9]   *VCH Middlesex,* Vol. V, 114-115.
[10]   *Ibid* 115.
[11]   *Ibid* 97.
[12]   *Ibid,* where details of the succession of leaseholders may be found.
[13]   London Metropolitan Archive, Acc. 262 17, Bundle 1.
[14]   LMA, Acc. 262 17, Bundle 1.
[15]   *VCH Middlesex,* Vol. V, 115.
[16]   LMA, Acc. 262 17.
[17]   LMA, Acc. 262 17, Bundle 1.
[18]   Daniel Defoe, *A Tour through the whole Island of Great Britain,* Letter 6 (1724).
[19]   *Ibid.*
[20]   LMA, Acc. 262 17, Bundle 1.
[21]   *Ibid.*
[22]   *Ibid.*
[23]   Sale Particulars, Canons Park 1920 (Harrow Civic Centre Library).
[24]   Sale Particulars, Bentley Priory 1909 (Harrow Civic Centre Library).

**The Parish Church of Great Stanmore**
[1]   LMA, DRO 14/B2/23-42, Letters and papers relating to building of new church.
[2]   *Ibid.*

[3]   LMA, Acc. 398/11.
[4]   *Ibid,* DRO 14/A1/1.
[5]   *VCH Middlesex,* Vol. V, 107-108.
[6]   Davenport MS (Harrow Civic Centre Library).

**St Lawrence's Church**
[1]   *VCH Middlesex* Vol. V, 114
[2]   *Ibid,* 123
[3]   Druett, *op. cit.,* 88-89.
[4]   C.H.C. & M.I. Baker, *James Brydges....1st Duke of Chandos* (XXXX).
[5]   Michael Robbins, 'A Middlesex Diary' *Transactions of the London & Middlesex Archaeological Society* (1953).

**Life in Rural Stanmore**
[1]   Extracted from the Bodleian Rental of 1306, transcribed in E.A. Webb's *The Records of St Bartholomew's, Smithfield.*
[2]   Druett, *op. cit.,* 33
[3]   Percy Davenport, *Old Stanmore,* (1933) 94
[4]   Davenport MS Court rolls Great Stanmore 1576 (Harrow Civic Centre Library).
[5]   LMA, Acc. 262 17, Bundle 1.
[6]   Druett, *op. cit.,* 64
[7]   Bodleian Rental *op. cit.*
[8]   LMA, Acc. 262 17, Bundle 1.
[9]   Davenport, *Old Stanmore,* 96.
[10]   *Ibid,* 105.
[11]   LMA, DRO 14 A1/1.

**Woods and Warren**
[1]   LMA, Acc 262, Bundle 1.
[2]   Davenport MS (Harrow Civic Centre Library).
[3]   LMA, MLR 1815, 2/383.
[4]   *VCH Middlesex,* Vol. V, 119
[5]   *Ibid.*
[6]   LMA, MLR 1815, 2/383.
[7]   *Ibid.* and Acc. 453/4/1A.
[8]   LMA, Acc. 262, Set 50/18.
[9]   Davenport MS.
[10]   LMA, Acc 262 17, Bundle 1.
[11]   Davenport MS.
[12]   LMA, Acc 262 17, Bundle 1.

**'Beset with Gentlemen's Houses'**
[1]   *Letters of William Morris,* ed. P. Henderson (in Stanmore Houses File at Harrow Civic Centre Library).
[2]   LMA, MLR 1815, 2 383
[3]   *Ibid.*
[4]   Daniel Lysons, *The Environs of London ....* , Vol. II, 665 (1811).
[5]   *Ibid.*
[6]   LMA, MLR 1815, 2 383
[7]   *Ibid.*
[8]   LMA, Acc 658/5, 77 and 113.
[9]   LMA, MLR 1835, 5 701.
[10]   This and succeeding paragraphs, LMA Acc. 531/11 and 12.

[11] *Letters of William Morris op. cit.*
[12] LMA, Acc. 502/50.
[13] LMA, Acc. 502/50-53.
[14] LMA, Acc. 531.
[15] Painting reproduced in Alan W. Ball, *The Countryside lies Sleeping* (1981).
[16] LMA, MLR 1813, 9 271.
[17] *Ibid*, MLR 1822, 3 489.
[18] Acc. 658/5, 123
[19] This and succeeding paragraph, Druett, *op. cit.*
[20] This and succeeding paragraph, Stanmore Houses file (Harrow Civic Centre Library).
[21] LMA, Acc. 262, Bundle 1.
[22] *Ibid*, Acc. 788/12.
[23] *Ibid*, Acc. 262/23: Humphrey Ward's photocopy.
[24] LMA, Acc. 658/6.
[25] This and following: Sale Particulars of Vaillant's property 1803, at Harrow Civic Centre Library.
[26] Sale Particulars, Stanmore Hall 1888 at Harrow Civic Centre Library.

### The Grove and The Limes
[1] This and following from Davenport MS and Stanmore Houses file at Harrow Civic Centre Library.
[2] Stanmore Houses file as above.

### Houses on Stanmore Hill
[1] This and following from LMA, Historical Notes 14/5/1970.
[2] LMA, Acc. 883/38b
[3] LMA, Acc. 883/33
[4] LMA, Acc. 503/58.
[5] Sale Particulars of Woodlands, 1899 at Harrow Civic Centre Library.

### Two Great Houses
[1] *VCH Middlesex*, Vol. IV, 206; Druett, *op. cit.* 102.
[2] Druett, *op. cit.* 105.
[3] *VCH Middlesex*, Vol. IV, 206.
[4] Druett, *op. cit.* 105.
[5] Statutory Declaration by Earl of Aberdeen 1853, quoted in Sales Particulars of Bentley Priory, 1880 at Harrow Civic Centre Library.
[6] *VCH Middlesex* Vol. V, 98
[7] LMA, Acc. 502/51.
[8] Sale Particulars of Bentley Priory 1880, at Harrow Civic Centre Library.
[9] St Bartholomew's Hospital Archives: Governors' Journal 1854-60.

[10] *Ibid*.
[11] LMA, Acc. 502/10.
[12] Jean Linwood, 'Bentley Priory' in *Stanmore & Harrow History Society Newsletter*, 1992.
[13] Alan W. Ball, *The Countryside lies sleeping* (1981).
[14] Much of the information in this paragraph is from Isabel Thompson, 'Andrew Drummond and Stanmore Park: Where was Hodgkins?' in *The Salubrious Air* (1993).
[15] File cards at Harrow Civic Centre Library.
[16] Alan W. Ball, *op. cit.*
[17] File cards at Harrow Civic Centre Library.

### Growing Villages
[1] This and following, LMA, DRO 14/C1/4
[2] Audrey Chamberlain, *Goodbye Gore* (1986).
[3] LMA, MRC L.
[4] *VCH Middlesex*, Vol. V, 120-121.
[5] This and following, LMA, DRO 14/C1/2.
[6] *Harrow Observer*.
[7] LMA, DRO 14/C1/2.
[8] *Ibid*.
[9] *Ibid*, DRO 14/C1/2 and DRO 14/F1/1.
[10] *Ibid*, DRO 14/F4/2-5.
[11] *Ibid*, DRO 14/F1/1 and C1/4.
[12] *Ibid*, DRO 14/F2/1.
[13] *Ibid*, DRO 14/F3/1 and F1/1.
[14] *Ibid*, BG H/1 and H/2.

### The Stanmores in Victorian Times
[1] *VCH Middlesex*, Vol. V, 99.
[2] LMA, Acc. 488.

### Passing the Time
[1] *VCH Middlesex*, Vol. V, 102.
[2] Sales Brochure, Stanmore Hall, 1888 (Harrow Civic Centre Library).
[3] Jill Moorhouse, Glebe Hall.

### Local Essentials
[1] Druett, *op. cit.* 250-1.
[2] *VCH Middlesex*, Vol. V, 105.

### The Leafy Suburb
[1] St Bartholomew's Hospital Archives: Journal 1854-60.
[2] LMA, Acc. 488.
[3] Tetlow et al *Bentley Priory – a history* (1996).

# Index

Asterisks denote illust-
rations and captions